The Sunday After Tuesday

The Sunday After Tuesday

College Pulpits Respond to 9/11

Compiled and Edited by
William H. Willimon

Afterword by
Stanley M. Hauerwas

Abingdon Press / Nashville

THE SUNDAY AFTER TUESDAY
COLLEGE PULPITS RESPOND TO 9/11

Copyright © 2002 by Abingdon Press

This book is printed on acid-free, recycled, elemental-chlorine–free paper.

Library of Congress Cataloging-in-Publication Data

The Sunday after Tuesday : college pulpits respond to 9/11 / compiled and edited by William H. Willimon ; afterword by Stanley M. Hauerwas.
    p. cm.
    ISBN 0-687-02838-8 (pbk. : alk. paper)
    1. September 11 Terrorist Attacks, 2001—Sermons. 2. Universities and colleges—Sermons. 3. Sermons, American—21st century. I. Willimon, William H.
    BT736.15 S86 2002
    252—dc21

                                        2001007617

"Outer Turmoil, Inner Strength," by Peter Gomes (chapter 12), first appeared in a slightly different form in *9.11.01: African American Leaders Respond to an American Tragedy*, edited by Martha Simmons and Frank A. Thomas. Valley Forge, PA: Judson Press, 2001.

Discussion guide by Rebecca Laird

02 03 04 05 06 07 08 09 10 11—10 9 8 7 6 5 4 3 2 1

MANUFACTURED IN THE UNITED STATES OF AMERICA

In memory of
Catherine "Cat" Fairfax MacRae,
2000 Graduate of Princeton University,
and all the young adults who died on September 11

Contents

Introduction

Preaching After Tuesday

The Desire for a Word—Within Limits

A trauma such as we endured on that fateful Tuesday (September 11, 2001) makes intellectuals of us all. Such a dramatic severance from all that reassures us compels each to ask, Why?

After Tuesday, for a time at least, it seemed as if everybody had to be a theologian whether one wanted to be a theologian or not. "God, why?"

But many of us found that one had to be a theologian within certain restraints. It is socially acceptable to ask, Why? To be a bit more specific of our cultural context, it is quite conventional to ask, Why did this happen to *me?*

What is risky, potentially unacceptable are the possible answers to that question. In the face of a devastating national crisis, it was a time to pull together, to move as one, we were told, not a time for second-guessing, nay-saying, or national self-critiquing.

The old Roman Imperial families knew enough to expel

all of their Greek philosophers during times of civil strife or national threat. During such times, when the omnipotence of Rome is imperiled, philosophers, with their incessant questions, can be a real nuisance. When the Empire is in jeopardy, solidarity is required, not potentially divisive critical questioning, much less sober reflection and honesty. There must be a united front against the enemy.

Thus, in the week after Tuesday, we experienced two conflicting tendencies. One sees that twofold conflict in this collection of sermons.

On the one hand, we were desperate for a word, an answer to the question, Why? In thirty years of ministry, I do not recall seeing people so desperate for words. In the days following, I had calls from the BBC, NBC, and from a number of local news stations curious about what clergy were saying after Tuesday. *The New York Times* reprinted excerpts from sermons around the city the next week. A great trauma makes theologians of us all. In the face of so massive a tragedy, we become desperate for the Word. More than one fellow preacher told me that, after spending a lifetime complaining that no one listens to preachers, it was truly terrifying suddenly to be thrust into a moment when everyone wanted to hear a sermon. As I stood on the steps of our university chapel that Sunday, looking into the faces of those scurrying in—a good half hour before the service was to begin—I saw on their faces desperation. And I—as the only person at the chapel that day who knew what the sermon intended to say—panicked.

On the other hand, while people seemed to desperately want a word, there were plenty of indications that the word we wanted would be carefully policed.

Politically Incorrect TV talk show host Bill Maher was severely censored for his rather flippant comments about the terrorists, saying that they were brave—crazy but brave—braver than the United States who merely sent unmanned missiles at our adversaries. Maher was forced to apologize profusely.

When newscaster Peter Jennings expressed the mildest of reservations about the president's rhetorical abilities, thousands of emails rebuked him.

It was a time for the country to unite, not a time for naysaying. In a moment we had all been rendered victims, not just those of us in New York, but all Americans. A great injustice can produce a great sense of innocence among those who have suffered the injustice. Innocence is particularly dangerous when it is felt among the powerful, because the powerful can be terribly destructive when they believe themselves to be innocent. When one is a pure victim, totally innocent, then all moral bets are off. Ships were sent to sea to guard Manhattan.

"Bomb 'em to hell," chanted a small group of students on Wednesday after a memorial service on our campus for the victims.

The service on Friday after Tuesday, at the National Cathedral, appeared to set the tone for many services throughout the country. The service was relentlessly patriotic, with little word of judgment or even reservation expressed by the clergy. President Bush stood in the pulpit and called for all-out war and retribution. At Robert Schuller's Crystal Cathedral, they unfurled the flag. And everyone seemed eager to stand and sing "God Bless America." The predominant symbol for the week that stands out in everyone's mind was the American flag, not the Christian cross.

I received an email from a sophomore on Sunday evening, after what I thought had been a wonderful service in our chapel that morning. The sophomore was "deeply disappointed" that there was hardly any mention of support for "our president" in the service, and "even more disturbing, a total absence of our beloved flag." "You politically correct clergy have failed to help us during our crisis," he complained.

I explained to the young man, as best I could, that this was church, not Yankee Stadium, that we have been given resources greater than the innocuous TV platitudes like "UNITY," "TOGETHER," and "FORWARD." I told him that on Sunday between eleven o'clock and noon we had our hands full just trying to listen to Jesus, just bending our lives toward him, so by noon there tended to be no energy left for support of the president. It wasn't that the church and its clergy were "politically correct," it was just that we were strange. We hoped that it was following Jesus that made us that way.

I haven't seen this student in the chapel since.

As a young pastor in Switzerland, Karl Barth said that he felt stretched between the contemporary situation and the biblical text. How to speak a word between the two? "As ministers we ought to speak of God. We are human, however, and so cannot speak of God. We ought therefore to recognize both our obligation and our inability and by that very recognition give God glory."[1] Many of us preachers found that, when faced with so huge an event as September 11, the situation at the moment tended to elbow God out of the way. In Florida, at a large service that following Sunday, the preacher called for "massive and disproportionate retaliation" upon any nation that colludes with terrorists, saying that when the Army caught the terrorists, the terrorists ought to be executed on the spot. His comment was greeted, it was reported, with amens and hallelujahs.[2]

The Strangeness of Peculiarly Christian Worship

This is where we preachers come in. On Sunday after Tuesday, it was our peculiar task not simply to comfort a people in trauma, but to comfort in the name of Jesus Christ. Our business was not simply to offer a helpful word, but a faithful one as well. Laying the story of the life, death, and resurrection of Jesus over the story of September 11 was our great challenge by September 16.

How well did we clerical workers in words do when the world was desperate for a word? By reading these sermons that were given to mostly twenty-something listeners, you can judge for yourself. The sermons represent a rather amazing breadth, and sometimes even depth, of American Christian pulpit work. In these sermons you will look over the shoulders of pastors at work attempting to help their young listeners think through the intellectual and theological challenges of the present hour. You will encounter a sort of barometer of American church life. I also hope that you will be edified and strengthened for the challenges of a world that is still learning not only the significance of what happened on a Tuesday morning in New York and Washington, but also the significance of what happened in Jerusalem on a Friday at noon.

A few impressions after collecting these sermons:

My impression was that many congregations that lacked substantive liturgical habits lacked the theological means to resist the pressures of the moment. When in great pain we reached for a reassuring symbol, we grasped an American flag, not a chalice or a Bible. It is therefore probably not amazing that some of these sermons offer mostly humanistic advice, patriotic suggestions for things that we can do to take away some of the pain rather than reach for an affirmation about what God has done or is doing in the present crisis. Some of the sermons seem greatly concerned to somehow account for all that God did *not* do in the crisis.

All of these sermons are preached by campus pastors, chaplains, or pastors who work with students. One of the characteristics of this generation of young adults is their ambivalence, or downright hostility, toward institutional, traditional embodiment of the faith. They tend to prefer something vaguely reassuring, like "spirituality," to the more demanding, more specific orthodox Christian faith. So it is not surprising to find those who speak to them invoking the values of friendship, caring, volunteerism, and personal involvement rather than more theologically explicit commitments.

What is amazing is that most of these sermons really try to stand under a biblical text, really struggle theologically with "Is there any word from the Lord?" In so doing, they preach from an amazing diversity of texts. We have sermons here on texts that range from the Tower of Babel to 1 Corinthians 13. For my sermon that Sunday, I immediately jettisoned the prescribed Common Lectionary texts and went with Genesis 1. Yet there is much to be said for those who stayed with a text prescribed by the lectionary on the Sunday after Tuesday and let the text rather than Tuesday determine the thrust of the sermon. I found a peculiar delight in the sermons that, while clearly shaped by the events of the week, were not utterly determined by them, were not jerked around by either the terrorists or the politicians, and went on and preached the great themes of the faith. This in itself became a kind of testimonial that the church rather than the world sets the agenda for the people of God.

Karl Barth, when in an article for *The Christian Century* in 1939 he testified to how his mind had changed, almost apologetically explained that while he was busy doing theology, Hitler came on the scene. Hitler's ascendancy made it necessary for him, for the moment, to lay aside more pressing churchly concerns and become "*simultaneously,* very much more churchly *and* very much more worldly. . . . For this change I am indebted to the Führer!"[3] Perhaps we preachers to young adults—thrust so suddenly to the forefront by a world demanding a word, by the rhetorical shortfall of the president, by the fury of the terrorists, by the bundle of feelings of hurt, hate, and loss—ought to express our gratitude to the world for suddenly making the peculiar speech of the church once again a matter of life and death.

Our chapel was packed to capacity in the weeks after the tragedy on Tuesday. Since that time, as the war has become almost routine, and the terrorist threat more diffused, the congregation has dwindled to more typical proportions. What, that first Sunday, seemed like a people turning desperately back to God has become a people following the president's exhortation to get back to business as usual. Thus, I have been reminded these past weeks that it is not an easy thing, certainly not a thing that comes naturally, to worship the true and living God.

A friend of mine was briefly on a nationwide radio talk show, appearing there as a "Christian representative." The interviewer told each participant that he or she would have only about two minutes to speak. When the show began, the interviewer turned to my friend and said, "Now you are a pastor. Tell us, what does your faith say about what we've been through?"

My friend cleared his throat and said something like, "Well, as Christians we are trying to follow Jesus, who forgave his enemies and refused to let us defend him. Jesus also teaches us that we are all sinners; even when we are wronged by others, we are like them in our sin. So we ask God to forgive us and to help us see even our enemies as brothers and sisters in Christ."

"Thank you," said the host. Then he turned to the next guest with, "Rabbi, what does your faith say about what we've been through?"

"First, let me say that I totally disagree with what your first guest just said. That's terrible! We don't need this sort of wishy-washy forgiveness bit. We need strong response to these terrorists. That's all they understand. Those people who died were not 'sinners,' they were victims of inhuman aggression."

Well, it's a time to be reminded of how very strange is the gospel.

It is a very peculiar thing to worship the true and living God, a God who comes to us as Trinity, a God who is a Jew from Nazareth. As one of our preachers puts it, "I am a member of a religion that worships a Middle Eastern man." So, as one of the endless TV interpreters of Islam, the professor who said that "Christians and Moslems all worship the same God" did not get it quite right. The same God may be a theoretical possibility but is not an actuality, if you care about being faithful to the Bible. Jesus does not easily mesh with Muhammad, no matter how much our need for national unity. There is a rather remarkable gulf between Islam and Christianity and, in deference to both faiths, that difference must be respected. One can only wonder what Bin Laden and his cohorts think of George Bush lecturing them on "true Islam."

A couple of Sundays after our fateful Tuesday, while attending a large downtown church, I noticed that the young children were entering the sanctuary for the service with bags marked "Worshiper in Training." In our place, we called those same children's activity bags, full of crayons, Bible coloring books, and so forth, "Quiet Bags." I like better the designation "Worshiper in Training" not only for the children, but for us all. On any Sunday morning, in any church, all of us are constantly in training for the odd activity of worshiping a God of truth and light. Faithful Christian worship is always a challenge but never so great as when we walk to church through the rubble of dashed dreams, crushed innocence, the end of the old world, and the uncertain, even frightening beginning of the new.

An associate preached a sermon a couple of weeks later in which he told of a conversation with a Duke student. The student's little brothers, aged something like six and four, were being kept by their father on the Wednesday after Tuesday. The father was trying to baby-sit and listen to the television news at the same time. The TV announcer said that the president was going to address the nation in just a moment.

"Now you and your brother have got to be quiet because the most important person in the world is getting ready to speak!" said the father to the older of the two children.

The six-year-old turned and said to his brother, "You have got to be quiet now. God is about to speak to us." Out of the mouths of babes.

It is unsurprising that many of these sermons are mostly in a therapeutic mode, including my own. Just five days after the tragedy, people were still in acute pain and shock. It did not seem a time for prophetic judgment, but a time for pastoral reassurance. What I found rather amazing is that a number of these sermons go right ahead and wade into matters of judgment. While their interpretations have more theological nuance than the early statements of Jerry Falwell or Pat Robertson, some of these preachers are so brash as to interpret the events that happened on September 11 as testimony to the sin not only of the terrorists, but our sin as well. Perhaps these campus pastors knew that there can be no real healing without truthful ministry to the cognitive dissonance that was felt by many after Tuesday. We were in a new world. New thinking was required. And an integral part of any specifically *Christian* thinking is going to be confession, repentance, forgiveness, acceptance of responsibility, honesty, speaking the truth in love, and all the other peculiar virtues that are part of Christian worship.

Making Meaning Among the Millennials

The sermons in this collection are preached by pastors, professors, and campus ministers to students, not exclusively, but predominantly young adult congregations. They thus provide a picture of one generation attempting to help another make sense of a world that has shifted on its axis. I am sure that it is as yet too soon to make sure generalizations about the future course of this young adult generation. Yet I have, from my vantage in the middle of a university, a few hunches.

For sometime many of us in campus ministry have lamented the civic disengagement and political apathy of our

21

students. On our campus, the last two national elections came and went with scarcely a ripple of interest among our students. Tuesday may have thrust them into politics. Or the uncertainty, the complexity of the new world may have entirely overwhelmed them, driven them into even greater self-absorption. I don't yet know. People who have suffered a great shock, a great grief, are not, in my pastoral experience, the type of folk who rush out to take on the challenges of the world.

Some of our students desperately want to believe that our national leaders are up to the task that is set before them, if we just give them our wholehearted support. But President Bush is my age. In my experience, this generation of young adults has little trust in my generation. In their book *Millennials Rising: The Next Great Generation,*[4] William Strauss and Neil Howe attempt to characterize America's youngest generation, those who were born after 1980 and who now populate our campuses. These veteran observers of students tell us that the best way to characterize the millennials "is as a correction for the boomers—that is, many of the things boomers were not, they are."[5] These children of the children of the 1960s have tended to be sheltered, parentally protected, optimistic, perfectionistic, closely attached (by way of cell phones) to their parents, and ultra-organized, putting a high premium on personal safety and regarding college as a safe, well-manicured garden apart from the messiness of the world. They have thus tended to embody many of the desires and values that their boomer parents do not.

Note that I have been speaking in the past tense. Reading back through Strauss and Howe's book, in preparation for this introductory essay, I had the distinct feeling that they were describing a generation that may be in radical metamorphosis. If it is true, and I think it is, that this generation has put a high premium upon security, lack of risk, and perfect parental protection, then they were wrong. Tuesday may have rocked them in a profound way. Now, as they are called up for active military duty in a still frighteningly ill-defined war; as the economy sinks and the good-paying first jobs vanish; as national leaders admit that they cannot guarantee the security of our lives or even of our mail, I expect we will witness some great changes among the millennials. Strauss and Howe will be forced to rethink their generational generalizations, as will we all.

What does it mean for the future of this generation that Tuesday is destined to be the defining event for their lives? I recall Harvard's Arthur Levine, who has spent a lifetime studying young adults, saying that when my generation thought "space exploration," we boomers thought of John Glenn going up against the Russians. But when the students of the 1990s thought about space, they pictured a school-teacher being blown up in spaceship *Challenger*. Levine's observations suggested to me that I was not living in the same assumptive world as a student of the 1990s. What will it mean for the assumptive world of today's young adults, the millennials, that their definitive image will be either a huge tower cascading to earth in a hail of rubble, or hate-filled terrorists dive-bombing a passenger jet into a symbol of our national pride? Or will their emblem be courageous fire-fighters clawing through the rubble searching for victims? Through what lens will they look at the world?

Any Sunday, but especially the Sunday after Tuesday, is in great part a struggle over the question, Who gets to name what's going on in the world? Who gets to say what is real? Through what lens, what focal image will we make sense out of the world as it presents itself to us—raw, dissonant, demanding—to be interpreted?

Preaching is one aspect of being a worshiper in training. Part of the preaching task is to keep laying the narrative that is the gospel over the booming, buzzing, confusion of life. Through the matrix of the gospel, we keep trying to look at the world through the peculiar lens of Scripture to read our circuitous story into God's providential story, to inquire

23

amid the cacophony of contemporary interpreters, Is there any word from the Lord?

Thus we listen in on a group of preachers, campus ministers, attempting to speak God's good news after a week of terribly bad news. We look over the shoulders of a group of adults attempting to help young adults make their way through the rubble. By what words did some of our best preachers attempt to proclaim the Word on the Sunday, that fateful Sunday, after so fateful a Tuesday?

Special thanks to Ms. Jacqueline Andrews for her invaluable assistance in collecting these sermons and preparing them for publication.

William H. Willimon
Duke University Chapel
Durham, North Carolina
Advent I

Notes

1. Karl Barth, *The Word of God and the Word of Man* (1926), p. 186.
2. Jeffrey DeYoe, "Homegrown Extremism: Preaching in Daytona Beach," *The Christian Century*, October 10, 2001, p. 7.
3. Karl Barth, "How My Mind Has Changed in This Decade: Part Two," *The Christian Century*, September 29, 1939, p. 684.
4. Neil Howe and William Strauss, *Millennials Rising: The Next Great Generation* (New York: Morrow, 1991).
5. William Strauss, interviewed by John Wesley Lowery, "The Millennials Come to Campus," *About Campus*, July-August 2001, p. 7.

One

Been There; Done That

Luther C. Alexander, Jr.
United States Naval Academy Chapel

Who knows the grief of a thirty-five-year-old widow? Who knows the anguish of a waiting parent? Who knows the struggle of good versus evil? Who knows—*really* knows—except someone who has been there?

While this week's events are as historic as they are troubling, "infamous days" are not unknown to America in her two-hundred-twenty-five-year history. Within the last sixty years we have experienced numerous other crises that have tried our patience and tested our commitment to the stated principles upon which this nation was founded.

From Pearl Harbor to the Cuban Missile Crisis; from the assassination of John F. Kennedy to the Vietnam War; from the 1987 stock market crash to the Gulf War to last year's presidential elections—as a nation, we have *been there.*

Not only have we visited scientific, economic, diplomatic, political, and military frontiers but, by the grace of God, we have returned "home" flush with satisfaction. As is so often the case today, bumper stickers announce our critique: "Been there; done that; got the T-shirt."

Yet our strength as a nation is inextricably tied to our devotion as individuals. Righteous governments do not exist apart from righteous individuals. Moral decisions in combat must originate with military and civilian leaders who themselves are moral. Gracious acts in our homes, in the workplace, in the classroom, and in the Brigade come only from gracious people. The Latin phrase is, *Nemo dat quod non habet:* You cannot give what you do not have.

In these critical days, the secret, spiritual contribution of devoted men and women is no less important than the public, tangible contributions of steelworkers and heavy equipment operators. While human effort can rebuild cities, only God can heal a broken spirit.

We need not go looking for these challenges. As night follows day, the challenges will find us!

One challenge that has already come to us is racism. Already, some of our shipmates and fellow citizens—whose only "offense" is the spelling of their name or their ancestral country—have been the target of slurs and other abuse. Muslim houses of worship in our country have received bomb threats. *Americans* of Arabic descent are considered guilty until proved innocent.

As disciples of Jesus, we must live the truth. The truth is this: judging Islam and its adherents by terrorist Osama Bin Laden is like judging Christianity by white supremacist David Duke.

The eighteenth-century English writer Samuel Johnson wrote: "Patriotism is the last refuge of a scoundrel." The same may be said of religion. Yet the Word of God—in both the Old and New Testaments—says: "Love your neighbor as [much as you love] yourself" (Leviticus 19:18; James 2:8 NIV).

This week will you be the reasonable voice, or will you remain silent? When the slander begins, will you let your light shine, or will you hide it under a basket?

Another such challenge is idolatry. Anytime we replace God with something or someone, it's idolatry. When we are threatened, who (or what) is our refuge? When we are afraid, to whom (or what) do we run?

There are two critical times in life when the disciple of Christ is tempted by idolatry: when times are good and when times are bad. In good times we are tempted to forget God and his faithfulness to us. In bad times we want a cure. These are bad times, but don't jump ship. The psalmist put it this way:

> God is our refuge and strength,
>   an ever-present help in trouble.
> Therefore we will not fear, though the earth give way
>   and the mountains fall into the heart of the sea,
> though its waters roar and foam
>   and the mountains quake with their surging. (Psalm 46:1-3)

Meeting these challenges requires something of each of us that is very simple but very costly: to *want* to be like Christ.

To want to be like Christ requires us to love our enemies— all of them. Jesus put it this way: "Love your enemies, do good to those who hate you, bless those who curse you, pray for those who mistreat you" (Luke 6:27-28 NIV).

Do you have enemies? Jesus knows what it's like to have enemies; his enemies successfully conspired to murder him.

Are you weeping? Jesus knows what it's like to weep; he wept while in spiritual agony before he was crucified. He wept at the tomb of his friend Lazarus. He wept for his people and their indifference to God's will.

Are you dismayed by the twistedness of some people? Jesus knows what it's like to have a relative die in a violent act; his cousin John the Baptist was decapitated to settle a grudge.

He's been there! He's done it all! He knows our situation because he's been in our situation. More than that, he offers to guide us from despair to hope; from sorrow to joy; uncertainty to victory; from death to life.

Jesus alone is worthy of our trust. If you are seeking security, he is security. If you are seeking comfort, he is the source of all comfort. If you are seeking rest, he says, "Come to me, all you who are weary and burdened, and I will give you rest. Take my yoke upon you and learn from me, for I am gentle and humble in heart, and you will find rest for your souls. For my yoke is easy and my burden is light" (Matthew 11:28-30 NIV).

If the Spirit of God is speaking to you today, don't be silent. Talk back. *Wanting* to be like Jesus is the first step toward *becoming* like Jesus. If you want to accept his offer of true salvation, the Bible says to confess with your mouth that Jesus is Lord and believe in your heart that God has raised him from the dead (Romans 10:9).

Yesterday, my family and I made a road trip to Rehoboth Beach in Delaware. All along the one-hundred-mile route were American flags and signs. Most commonly the sign would say, "God bless America." As our strength as a nation is inextricably tied to our devotion as individuals, the blessings of God come to a nation through the people of God.

God has blessed America, and God desires to continue blessing America—through you and me. The challenge is *before* us. The challenge will *find* us. How will you respond?

Two

Our Challenge Now

Dave Ball
Service of Remembrance and Healing
Denison University

Three weeks ago today we awoke to the shocking news that a fellow student, a friend of ours, had left us, never to return.

Ever since, we have been grasping—grasping to understand how he could decide to take his own life; grasping for some way to cope with our sadness at losing him, and with our own frustration that we had not seen this coming and intervened.

Nearly two weeks had passed, and we were still grasping for closure, when a Tuesday that I expected to be pretty normal, all things considered, became a day of unforgettable horror and tragedy, which only became worse the more we heard about and learned about those who had died.

Tragedy this close to home, and tragedy of this magnitude, have brought out perhaps the finest human impulse in us: the desire to do something in response to these tragedies that, since we can't relive the past and prevent them, will at least allow us to gather as a community to express, in a rich and heartfelt way, how much we care about what has happened.

Nearly one hundred forty years ago, Americans gathered in response to this very same impulse at Gettysburg National Cemetery, at the Civil War battlefield where more than forty thousand to fifty thousand lives were lost.

Our anger at the loss of four thousand to five thousand civilian lives due to terrorist attacks must have surely been matched by [nineteenth-century Americans'] sadness over ten times that number of deaths—half from the North and half from the South, killed by their fellow countrymen.

And so President Abraham Lincoln commended them for gathering:

> We have come to dedicate a portion of . . . a great battle-field of that war . . . as a final resting place for those who here gave their lives that . . . [this] nation [—conceived in Liberty, and dedicated to the proposition that all . . . are created equal] might live. It is altogether fitting and proper that we should do this.

No sooner had Lincoln acknowledged the nobility of our human impulse to gather and remember the dead, however, than he elevated that impulse, above its role in prompting the present gathering, and sent it soaring toward the noblest future: "We can not dedicate—we can not consecrate—we can not hallow—this ground." That has already been done: "The brave men, living and dead, who struggled here, have consecrated it, far above our poor power to add or detract."

No, although our impulse to honor the dead has brought us here, there is nothing we can do to honor them by gathering. We can only adequately honor them by how we *live* from now on:

> It is for us the living, rather, to be dedicated here to the unfinished work which they who fought here have thus far so nobly advanced. It is rather for us to be here dedicated to the great task remaining before us [—that of ensuring that] "these dead shall not have died in vain—that this nation . . .

[dedicated to the proposition that all are created equal] shall have a new birth of freedom—and . . . shall not perish from the earth.

Lincoln took our human impulse to do something, if only to gather to remember the dead, and elevated it to the level of a commitment higher than which I cannot conceive, to ensure that the dead shall not have died in vain.

Their task, then, as framed by Lincoln's address, was clear: to rededicate themselves to the cause for which the Union soldiers had died—the defense of a nation where all are to be treated as equals.

Were we to emulate that gathering at Gettysburg and seek to ensure that *these* dead shall not have died in vain, however, our task would not be so clear, for these did not die for any single, unifying cause.

Our challenge now, if we seek to live up to as lofty a commitment as that which Lincoln held out for the Gettysburg gathering, will first be to figure out, as a community, what cause it would be to which we might dedicate ourselves.

It is not so clear-cut as completing "the unfinished work," which the Union soldiers had "so nobly advanced" at Gettysburg. Their clarity of purpose had emerged over decades of abolitionist ferment, seeking the end of slavery. We do not have the benefit of decades spent formulating and forging a common purpose appropriate to the problems we face.

But we cannot simply go back to business as usual. Our vice president has said, "I would hope the American people would . . . not let what's happened here in any way throw off their normal level of economic activity." Just to get back to work, without more, would be an affront to the memory of those who have died. Thus our challenge now, in response to this sudden tragedy, is to speed up the process of discovering and instilling a shared sense of purpose that would do honor to those who have died—through the application of our learning and critical thinking.

This is our challenge now, "that these dead shall not have died in vain." What will that high purpose be? It seems clear that U.S. foreign policy can no longer focus so exclusively on our own national interest—but how to frame a broader purpose, and how to bring about public support for it? Is our challenge still, as it was at the time of the Civil War, to create a community where all are to be treated as equals—broadening now from the national level to include the entire globe?

We, members of the Denison community, must be about this great unfinished task. This is our challenge to which we must turn—now.

Three

"Why Did This Happen?"

Darryl R. Barrow
Cannon Chapel, Emory University

Jesus answered, "You do not know now what I am doing, but later you will understand." (John 13:7)

For now we see in a mirror, dimly, but then we will see face to face. Now I know only in part; then I will know fully, even as I have been fully known. (1 Corinthians 13:12)

There are many things that happen to us in this life for which we can find no answer. Experiences we cannot understand baffle us. Take our present incomprehensible human tragedy and the distressing crisis we are facing. There sometimes seems to be no reason or purpose in what has taken place. In the dark hour of a great loss, sick with loneliness and anguish, anger and sorrow, our hearts cry out for an explanation. In such times we may find strength and guidance in the words of our Lord, spoken on the eve of the Crucifixion to the perplexed disciples—just as we are perplexed at this moment—in the upper room (John 13:7). These words speak to us as we confront the heaviest losses in our nation's history. They apply to us as we stand bereaved, puzzled, confused, mystified in the presence of events for which we can find no answer.

When we, as pastors, stand, as we often do, with heartbroken families after the sudden or tragic death of a family member or a close friend, we know that there is one reminder that may prove helpful to those who grieve. It is this: beyond the tragic event, an event that defies humanity's explanations, there is a purpose which faith alone can see amid the shadows and which patience will in time reveal. I submit to you that faith and patience will give strength and will give assurance of God's presence, purpose, power, and peace in our present trouble.

We live out our lives in the presence of mystery. There are so many experiences we cannot understand. We cry out for light:

> Behold, we know not anything;
>   I can but trust that good shall fall
>   At last—far off—at last, to all,
> And every winter change to spring.
>
> So runs my dream: but what am I?
>   An infant crying in the night:
>   An infant crying in the light:
> And with no language but a cry.
> (Alfred Tennyson, from *In Memoriam*)

If we could only be certain that this crushing blow is not from the hand of blind fate, but is permitted by a heavenly God who is "afflicted in all our afflictions!" We are not alone in our desire for assurance as we pass through the dark night of our soul: many people in each age have grappled with this matter. Out of this same state of mind and heart, however, have come some of the most beautiful and tender words of hope and guidance that have ever fallen upon the weary of heart as we grope in the shadows, even in the darkest shadows, of death. John Henry Newman, perplexed in mind and sick in body, wrote a hymn nearly two centuries ago that was to become the prayer for millions of people in each generation:

> Lead, kindly Light! amid the encircling gloom,
>   Lead thou me on;
> The night is dark, and I am far from home,
>   Lead thou me on.
> Keep thou my feet: I do not ask to see
> The distant scene; one step enough for me.
>
> So long thy power hath blest me, sure it still
>   Will lead me on,
> O'er moor and fen, o'er crag and torrent, till
>   The night is gone;
> And with the morn those Angel faces smile,
> Which I have loved long since, and lost awhile.
>   ("Lead, Kindly Light")

This is the prayer we offer to the many families and friends, and to the nation as a whole, affected by this terrible situation. In the hours of great anguish there is a question that comes back again and again to our minds. The query is summed up in the word *why*. How often do we hear persons, hear ourselves, say: *Why* did this happen? *Why* was this useful person taken? *Why* was this young person, so full of promise, cut off before the chance to make a contribution to life was granted?

Jesus knew well this word *why*. It was his word amid the darkness and anguish of Calvary. Out of the depths of an indescribable loneliness and desolation come the words, "My God, my God, *why* have you forsaken me?" In all of the Holy Scriptures there is no verse more difficult to explain. Surely the Lord was never closer to the suffering heart of humanity than when he uttered this cry. And the millions of *whys* that have arisen from agonized souls, jealous for the honor of God but perplexed by his providence, were concentrated in the *why* of Christ.

35

The final word from the cross may be, by the grace of God, our word. And for us also, as a people in pain and suffering, light may come out of our darkness, trust out of our uncertainty, and peace out of our anguish. "Father, into your hands I commend my spirit" (Luke 23:46).

I find the words of Elizabeth Browning appropriate here:

Yea, once Immanuel's orphaned cry his universe hath
    shaken—
It went up single, echoless, "My God, I am forsaken!"
It went up from the Holy's lips amid his lost creation,
That, of the lost, no son should use those words of
    desolation!

For my thoughts are not your thoughts,
    nor are your ways my ways, says the LORD. (Isaiah 55:8)

While life often confronts us with that which we can neither understand nor explain, yet life is not all mystery. If the unexplainable experiences of life are a terrific storm that blasts upon the citadel of faith, let us remember that that stronghold can be so constructed that it will not fall. Our great defense is trust in the goodness and wisdom of God.

For the Lord will not reject forever.
Although he causes grief, he will have compassion
    according to the abundance of his steadfast love
    [according to the multitude of his mercies];
for he does not willingly afflict or grieve anyone.
                    (Lamentations 3:31-33)

It was this confidence that grew in the heart of the apostle Paul, nourished on the presence and promises of Christ, that enabled him to say:

But we have this treasure in clay jars, so that it may be made
clear that this extraordinary power belongs to God and does

not come from us. We are afflicted in every way, but not crushed; perplexed, but not driven to despair; persecuted, but not forsaken; struck down, but not destroyed. (2 Corinthians 4:7-9)

But our citizenship is in heaven, and it is from there that we are expecting a Savior . . . [who] will transform the body of our humiliation that it may be conformed to the body of his glory. (Philippians 3:20-21)

"You do not know now what I am doing, but later you will understand."

And we shall see how all God's plans are right,
And what most seemed reproof was love most true.
(May Riley Smith, "Sometime")

Let us allow the God of truth and wisdom to speak, and let him form in us a true conscience. As he speaks to us, we need to hear and embrace his words, however difficult they may seem. We need his Holy Spirit and the higher wisdom that comes from his Spirit in order to love our enemies, do good to those who hate us, and pray for those who so brutally and irrationally maltreated us. Then and only then will we be a leaven of hope and love. Amen.

Four

In This Time of Crisis

Darrell Brazell
Wheatland Church of Christ
Lawrence, Kansas

In this time of crisis we must face the frailty of this life.

James 4:13-16 says this:

Now listen, you who say, "Today or tomorrow we will go to this or that city, spend a year there, carry on business and make money." Why, you do not even know what will happen tomorrow. What is your life? You are a mist that appears for a little while and then vanishes. Instead, you ought to say, "If it is the Lord's will, we will live and do this or that." As it is, you boast and brag. All such boasting is evil. (NIV)

Our life is but a mist. We naively believe that we have tomorrow and next week and next year. We think that we can do what we like today and make up for it tomorrow. We think we can work eighty hours this week and then spend a little extra time with our kids the next. We think we can work hard now and enjoy retirement later; yet later may never come.

On Tuesday morning, countless people went to work, left for vacation, went for a walk, or went shopping for the very last time. If they said good-bye to their families it was merely a formality; they had no idea that this time "good-bye" meant "good-bye."

If you have watched the news at all, you have seen countless individuals recount the final words someone they loved spoke to them.

Ecclesiastes 7:2 says, "It is better to go to a house of mourning than to go to a house of feasting, for death is the destiny of every man; the living should take this to heart" (NIV).

Those are difficult words. How can it be better to go to a house of mourning than a house of feasting? How? Because it forces us to face the frailty of this life and take every precious moment for what it is—a gracious gift from a loving heavenly Father. It reminds us that we cannot take this life for granted. In this time of crisis we must face the frailty of this life.

In this time of crisis we must face the futility of our idols. We must face our idol of wealth. In 1 Samuel 4 and 5, the Philistines capture the ark of God because the Israelites believe it can be used as a magical token ensuring their victory. Upon capturing the ark, the Philistines place it in the temple of their god, Dagon. The next morning, they arise to find their idol Dagon had fallen on his face before the ark of the Lord. No problem, just a coincidence. They place Dagon back on his feet.

However, the very next morning the Philistines find Dagon fallen again. This time, his hands and his head had broken off.

In many ways the World Trade Center can be seen as a modern Dagon. It was not targeted simply because of the height of its buildings. It was targeted because it is a symbol of American capitalism. While our currency says "In God We Trust," the reality is that America trusts in its financial stability. We trust in our credit cards, our bank accounts, and our retirement funds. Now, like Dagon, the idol has been toppled. Its hands and its head have crumbled. What value is there now to the six-figure income of the executive who worked eighty hours a week to keep his window office suite? What value is there now to all the Mercedes, BMWs, and high-priced SUVs that were parked below the towers?

Our Idol of Our Government

We too often place our trust in America and not in God. Even now, the temptation is to trust our military, to trust the FBI, to trust the FAA to make things safe again. Yes, there are things that they must do to improve security. Yes, there are things they must change to try to prevent such tragedies from happening again. However, it is not within our grasp to control the future. Only God knows and controls the future. Only God can see beyond right now. In fact, he is the only one who can truly see even now. Our vision is limited. Our resources are minuscule. Our power is but an illusion. Therefore we must turn to him and to him alone.

We are notorious for turning God's gifts into idols. He graciously gives us the ability to earn a living and provide for our families. Then we turn the gift of our job into an idol that we serve. God graciously gives us the income we need to put food on the table and a roof over our heads, and then we turn around and worship the house, the car, the savings account, the mutual fund, and the retirement account. God graciously has given us a government through which he protects and provides for us. Yet the temptation is to look to and place our trust in the government that God uses rather than the God who is above and beyond our government.

One question: When a crisis explodes our concept of reality, what value do our idols hold? What power to save do they contain? Times of crisis force us to face the futility of our idols.

In this time of crisis we must confess our sin. I cannot stand before you and tell you that Tuesday's tragedy is the judgment of God on America for its sins. I do not have that word from God.

However, we have countless examples from Scripture in which God uses ungodly men as instruments of discipline for his children. Judges 3:12 says: "Once again the Israelites did evil in the eyes of the LORD, and because they did this evil the LORD gave Eglon king of Moab power over Israel" (NIV). Also, Judges 4:1-2: "After Ehud died, the Israelites once again did evil in the eyes of the LORD. So the LORD sold them into the hands of Jabin, a king of Canaan, who reigned in Hazor" (NIV).

It is therefore possible that God is using the wicked men who masterminded this attack to bring us to repentance.

Listen to the words that God spoke to Solomon when Solomon had finished the Temple.

> I have heard your prayer and have chosen this place for myself as a temple for sacrifices. When I shut up the heavens so that there is no rain, or command locusts to devour the land or send a plague among my people, if my people, who are called by my name, will humble themselves and pray and seek my face and turn from their wicked ways, then will I hear from heaven and will forgive their sin and will heal their land. (2 Chronicles 7:12-14 NIV)

The first step of repentance is to confess our sin: confess our sins as a corporate nation; confess our sins as a corporate church; confess our sins as individuals.

In this time of crisis we must trust that God stands beside us. In the president's address on Friday at the Washington National Cathedral, he said this: "At St. Patrick's Cathedral in New York, on Tuesday, a woman said, 'I pray to God to give us a sign that he's still here.' "

Whenever there is suffering, whenever there is tragedy, the human tendency is to question the presence of God. *"Where is God when I suffer?"*

In times of crisis, Satan tells us to judge the character of God by our circumstances. Faith, however, tells us to judge our circumstances by the character of God. Romans 8:28 says: "And we know that in all things God works for the good of those who love him, who have been called according to his purpose" (NIV). Romans 8:38-39 says:

> For I am convinced that neither death nor life, neither angels nor demons, neither the present nor the future, nor any powers, neither height nor depth, nor anything else in all creation, will be able to separate us from the love of God that is in Christ Jesus our Lord. (NIV)

Satan tells us to look at the carnage, look at the death, look at the suffering and know that God is capricious; God is vengeful; God is distant. Faith, however, calls us to look at the cross and know that God is love. God understands suffering. He suffered for us. God understands pain, he endured the cross. God understands losing a loved one, for at the cross he had to forsake his own Son.

Even in our darkest hours, God stands beside us. In the words of David:

> Even though I walk
>   through the valley of the shadow of death,
> I will fear no evil,
>   for you are with me;
> your rod and your staff,
>   they comfort me. (Psalm 23:4 NIV)

In times of crisis we must trust that God stands beside us.

In this time of crisis we must seek the face of God. When I see the frailty of life, when I see the futility of my idols, all that is left is God. All that matters is whether I am rightly related to the Creator of the universe.

In God's words: "If my people, who are called by my name, will humble themselves and pray and seek my face and turn from their wicked ways, then will I hear from heaven and will forgive their sin and will heal their land" (2 Chronicles 7:14 NIV).

Brothers and sisters in Christ, and those of you who are not yet in Christ, you must think of the possibilities. You could have been on one of those planes. You could have been in one of those offices. One of those planes could have crashed into your home or your office. Today the attack could be here. Today it could be a bomb in this very building. There is no certainty to this life. Therefore if you are not in a saved relationship with Jesus Christ, today is the day to turn to God.

Today is the day to set aside your idols and accept God's free gift of salvation. Today is the day to exchange the uncertainty of this life for the certainty of eternal life that comes only through Jesus Christ.

Five

Putting Away Childish Things

Michael L. Budde
DePaul University

It seems that the time for what Kierkegaard called "playing church" has passed for Christians in North America. No longer is being a Christian a matter of make-believe, a comfortable and familiar role so easy that anyone can play and quit as it suits him or her. Christianity as a spectator sport has been canceled.

That the game is over is especially difficult to see now, amid the haze of burning buildings and the billowing of broadcloth flags. As the American government prepares for war—a war of punishment and retribution that is the special preserve of empires alone—clergy and laity alike bow in prayer for the victims and families, for shaken psyches and broken bodies, and for our rulers.

If it is hard to see that Christianity-as-hobby must be no longer, it is in part because the road chosen by the American state shines so brightly in illuminating our future. There will be war, but not just one war; there will be near-permanent, perpetual, pre-emptive war, interrupted by periods of calm while the planes rearm, the soldiers reload, and the ships refuel. By choosing vengeance and retribution in response to evil deeds, the American overseers have embarked on a path of war without end, amen.

In shock over the massive loss of life and the rude imposition of Third World violence into the economic and military symbols of the First, most churches are reverting instinctively to their role as chaplain and comforter—easing the pain of the survivors and bolstering the resolve of leaders planning for war. The chaplain's game is one in which the category of citizen trumps, swallows whole the theoretically more fundamental category of disciple.

Consider the prayer service for the nation's military and political leaders in Washington, D.C., on September 14. A veritable parliament of world religions—at least the big ones—attended and offered prayers and comfort, empathy and encouragement, to those whose duty to statecraft and the lethal arts made them deaf to the words in that day's lectionary. The cardinal archbishop of Washington proclaimed God's judgment that it is the meek, the peacemakers, and those who return good for evil who do God's will on earth— a most inconvenient text drawn from the church's worldwide calendar. No inconvenience or obstacle for those in attendance, however. No one seemed to mind that Billy Graham, bent and aged after years of counseling previous elected emperors—spoke not one word about the Gospel text of peacemaking and suffering rather than inflicting evil. In this game, no one thought it a glaring omission that Graham and The United Methodist minister who followed him made brief mention of "the nation's" need to repent of sin, without naming a single sin crying out for repentance or forgiveness.

Had they not been playing at Christianity, the august ministers could have named sin and sinners in abundance merely by working their way through the crowd. They could have found a list of sins and sinners broad enough to help explain hatred sufficient to drive jetliners into skyscrapers, and deep

enough to explain mercenaries now turned against their former paymasters—for that is the relationship between Bin
Laden and the American government. They could have
noted that September 11 is already occupied as a day of
mourning on some people's calendar—for those whose lives
were plunged into seventeen years of Pinochet's darkness,
after a U.S.–aided coup deposed the elected government of
Chile. September 11 is the Chileans' day no longer, for the
empire has need of it, will take it, and claim it henceforth.

A church of purpose rather than of play would have dared
interrogate that gathering of military, political, and economic power who listened to "God Bless America." Such a
church would ask what such a group meant in asking God to
"stand beside her, and guide her." Did God stand beside and
guide the nation as the nation installed murderous regimes
and dictators in Iran in 1953, Guatemala in 1954, Congo in
the early1960s, to name but a few? Did God stand beside and
guide America as it carpet bombed Vietnam, Laos, and
Cambodia; as it bankrolled fifty years of suffering in the
Middle East, ten years of starvation and disease in Iraq, and
death squads in too many countries to count? No church
worthy of the gospel would hang such a libel on God; but
one too confused to distinguish between church and Caesar
wouldn't know any other way. A church committed to God's
kingdom, one that refuses to divide the world into sectarian
political idolatries (otherwise known as patriotism and
nationalism, the former naming the latter when on its best
behavior), would refuse to play its bit part in a prayer service
filled with promises and foreshadowings of war. It would forever ban from its sanctuaries "The Battle Hymn of the
Republic," an appropriate closing hymn for a prayer service
for persons whose hearts leave still full of war.

Similar scenes play out elsewhere. In Chicago, the main
public moment of prayerful silence begins with the crowd
chanting "USA, USA, USA!"—a liturgy of self-assertion we
would see as proof of fanatical religious nationalism if done

in another country or as part of someone else's "religious" service. Across the nation, clergy have been summoned to pray for healing, but also for justice (as defined by the strong) and for wisdom (so that American retribution not cause undue damage to our self-image and self-interest).

The Chicago prayer service ends with those assembled in Daley Center Plaza—between ten thousand and twenty thousand people—waving flags as they sing "God Bless America." The unstated assumption here and across the country where this hymn echoes is that God will of course heed our request (or is it a demand?), thereby removing God's blessings from the people of Afghanistan or anyplace else due to suffer imperial revenge. Even God has been put on notice by the empire—get on our side, or get the hell out of the way.

Make no mistake, this will be a long war; and September 11 will be a blank check for American ambitions great and petty for the next several decades. Terrorism is a most useful enemy for the powerful, the recent surprise attack notwithstanding. We will see more money for the military and intelligence "community" (another chilling co-opting of language there), freedom to kill not only actual perpetrators of violence but also those that might do so in the future (the return of Reagan's "pre-emptive strike" authorization from the 1980s), and no need to fear domestic opposition to foreign adventures abroad. If Middle East groups can afford terrorism, so can "narco-terrorists" in Colombia and elsewhere; so can a potential world full of enemies that stand in the way of American political and economic objectives.

There is indeed a world full of poor and hurting people—pushed off their land, their wages driven down, their health and safety undermined. They are the collateral damage of the global market, of rules established and enforced by the United States and other wealthy countries through opaque institutions like the International Monetary Fund, the World Bank, and the World Trade Organization. The United States and its propertied groups benefit from these economic rules written to favor the privileged, rules that kill more people by way of preventable disease, malnutrition, and social unrest than do jetliners turned into assault vehicles. These slow-motion calamities, alas, lack dramatic video footage and the backdrop of the New York skyline. The losers in the world economy are expected to starve or waste away in quiet and polite obscurity; should they resist, be it in Latin America or Africa or Asia, they will now be even more vigorously surveilled and supervised lest they become an army of angry people possessed of nothing to lose and a handful of box cutters.

At my university, a public forum on the attack soon focused on the fear and insecurity of the school's large Muslim and Asian communities. Amid death threats, reports of assaults and the like, one frightened young woman asked what she and her fellow Muslim Americans could do to "prove our patriotism" to the rest of America. Many in the room of several hundred people reassured her that her patriotism was assumed, that being a good Muslim in no way conflicted with being a good American.

I tried unsuccessfully to gain the floor to raise one concern on the point, that the effectiveness of Christian assimilation to being a "good American" was precisely one major factor setting the table for the awful attack of September 11. Without Christians eager to do their patriotic duty, many of the most punishing exercises of American power in the world likely could not have happened, or happened as efficiently as they had. Were churches more serious about Jesus and his disavowal of the sword, the empire might have found its ability to project violence circumscribed if not undermined altogether. As it is, of course, most churches then and now bend over backward to prove their loyalty to the state— an expression of "radical Christian fundamentalism," if anyone had the courage to apply to ourselves the analytic frameworks we craft for our opponents of the day (for example, those "radical Islamic fundamentalists" that make the imperatives of organized power the obligation of God and God's followers).

If churches hope to be more than this, they will have to find the resources, practices, and language to define themselves as distinct from nation, state, and tribe. Churches will need to rediscover their integrity as real-world communities built upon mutuality, forgiveness, and peaceableness instead of coercion and common advantage. None of this is easy, even under the best of circumstances. As it is, it looks now to be played out in the long shadow of an unprovoked attack that will legitimate years of "just wars" to come.

One of the most corrosive effects of World War II, at least for the churches, was the memory of their unwaxed support for such a just war, it left most of them ill-equipped to resist the orders of leaders to follow, those who draped their more ambiguous ambitions with the warm mantle of the Good War. Only churches that understand the inescapable way of the cross are likely to achieve some clarity of vision in the years ahead, when every new exercise of American power will be glossed with pictures of airplanes, towers, and the heroic dead. To be a church that embraces the Beatitudes rather than ignores them—that requires people for whom being a Christian is not a game. It requires following Jesus and not generals.

Six

The Best of Times, the Worst of Times

Tony Campolo
Eastern College Chapel

> Once to every man and nation comes the moment to decide;
> In the strife of Truth with Falsehood, for the good or evil
> side;
> Some great cause, God's new Messiah, offering each the
> bloom or blight,
> . . . .
> And the choice goes by forever 'twixt that darkness and that
> light.
> ("The Present Crisis," James Russell Lowell, 1819–1891)

These are times that try our souls. They are the best of times; they are the worst of times. They are the best of times because we have seldom seen heroism in this country as we have seen over the last couple of weeks. As people were rushing out of the World Trade Center buildings because they were collapsing, firemen and policemen were rushing up the steps to see whom they could rescue, and it cost them their lives. We have seen daring commitments of faith.

It's the best of times because there's a new birth of patriotism in this country, and it's the kind I like. It's quite different from the patriotism of the Los Angeles Olympics, where we were waving our fingers in the faces of the rest of the world, yelling, "We're number one! We're number one! We're the best!" We're not saying that. We're not trying to exalt ourselves above anybody else. We're simply saying, "We're proud to be Americans." We embrace the values that have given this country birth. We are committed to the liberties, to the values, to the principles that have undergirded this country and made it great.

It's a time of altruism when Michael Jordan decides to not only come back but to say, "The millions of dollars I will make I am giving to the families of the victims." He can afford it, but that is a lot of money.

It's also the worst of times, because there are emotions that are emerging that we need to keep in check. For example, the profiling of Arab Americans. Please, people, we were just on the verge of getting rid of profiling. We were just about to wipe out racial profiling, and all of a sudden it rears its ugly head, and people are being ushered off of airplanes simply because they don't fit the profile of what the pilots think are decent Americans.

I worry about attitudes of vengeance. Vengeance is a very destructive mind-set. I hear the word *vengeance* over and over again. "Vengeance is mine; I will repay, saith the Lord" (Romans 12:19 KJV). We dare not usurp the prerogatives of God at a time like this. And may I point out that I differ with Senator McCain when he says, "God may give them mercy, but they'll get none from us." The truth is, I read a Bible that says, "Blessed are the merciful"; because if you're not merciful, you're not going to get any mercy. That's what the Bible says. Of all the senators I've heard speak, I thought Senator McClusky from Maryland said the best thing. In that great prayer meeting that they held under the Capitol dome, she said, "I pray, dear God, that you will bring those who perpetrated this evil"—and I was waiting for her to say "to justice," but she said—"to repentance." And that's our hope. If we

51

keep on returning evil for evil, violence for violence, we'll get nowhere. It's only when they and we come to repentance and we change our ways that a new day will dawn.

These can be the worst of times, if we don't ask the right questions. Here's the first one: *are we forgetting what Jesus told us?* Just a few days ago, after I had finished speaking, a man came up to me and said, "This is no time to go around quoting Jesus."

I've got news for you; this is exactly the time we had better quote Jesus. Let me tell you what Jesus said: "You have heard of old, 'An eye for eye and a tooth for tooth'; but I give you a new commandment. Do good to those who hurt you." I know somebody's going to say, "But in the Old Testament, that's the whole point." Jesus raises the ante, doesn't he? He creates an ethic that is superior to the Hebrew Bible when he calls us to return "good for evil." Doesn't he say that? Doesn't he say, "Return good for evil"? Does he not say that "those who live by the sword will die by the sword"? And that "violence begets violence"? And "Love your enemies"? Are we going to set that aside simply because it's inconvenient? Are we going to in fact say, "No way, we are not going to obey Jesus. We are not going to love our enemies; we are going to get vengeance on them"?

Here's what Jesus says, "If thine enemy hunger, feed him. If he's naked, clothe him. If he's sick, comfort him." I wonder what would happen if that became national policy. If instead of embargoing Iraq, we suddenly delivered tons and tons and tons of food to hundreds of thousands, yea, millions of children who are on the verge of starvation and death. I wonder what would happen if, as they are sick and dying without pharmaceutical supplies, we suddenly obeyed Jesus and ministered to the sick. I dare say this, that the embargo against Iraq and Afghanistan and Cuba has only strengthened those dictators. It has not brought them down. It has only solidified the resentment of the poor against the rich, and that's us.

The time has come for us to dare to be Christian. I know that 90 percent of the American population is for a quick military strike, but as Mark Twain once said, "When ninety percent of the population is for anything, you ought to stop and reflect." I contend this, that we ought to obey Jesus and, as Christians, we should urge our government to obey Jesus. It is time to quote a Jesus who said, "Blessed are the peacemakers." It's time to remember a scripture that says that we have been given a ministry of reconciliation. This is not an easy time to say such things. But we will be in the worst of times if we do not remember what Jesus told us.

Second question: *do we learn anything from history?* A thousand years ago there was a great conflict between so-called Christian nations and so-called Muslim nations—the Crusades. It's not surprising that the Muslim community has not forgotten the slaughter of millions and millions of people in the name of Jesus. And it is not surprising that Bin Laden invoked the Crusades and called upon Afghanistan's people and the Pakistani people to resist the Christian crusaders who would invade their land. The old rhetoric is back again.

I always remember what Saint Francis of Assisi did during the Crusades. He went down to Egypt on the eve of one of the most horrendous battles. He crossed the lines and left the Christian side and went into the Muslim camp. He went into the tent of the sultan and tried to tell him about a Jesus who loved him; he tried to convert the sultan to Christ. The sultan almost said, "I'll hear of this another day, but I have a battle to fight tomorrow." Francis said, "When you fight, many on both sides will die, and God will be the first to weep for those on both sides."

I've got a God who is not an American. I hate to say that right now. George Bernard Shaw said it well: "God created us in his image, and we decided to return the favor."

What have we learned from history? Are we going to have a rebirth of the Crusades? We haven't been able to do much in winning the Muslim world to Jesus Christ because of the Crusades. You know that. You know the impact we have had on the Muslim community has been nil, and I am here to tell you that Jesus Christ died for the Muslims just as much as he died for any one of us. And I need to affirm that. I ask you about Osama Bin Laden: have you prayed for that man today? Have you prayed that God would change his heart and change his mind? Or is your God too small to do such things?

As we go through these days I ask whether we learned anything from history. I mean, there was Vietnam. (I am old enough to remember; you're not.) The government promised us proof that Bin Laden and Afghanistan were responsible. Then yesterday they changed their minds and said, "We're not going to tell you." I've been on this route before. If they're going to ask one hundred thousand Americans to go over there and lay down their lives, they had better tell us what it's all about.

One of our own students has honored us by writing such a good letter to *Time* magazine. (So Eastern gets some good recognition in this.) He basically raised the question, Are we not like a soldier who pulls a pin out of a hand grenade and isn't quite sure where to throw it? Isn't that exactly our posture today? Please, this is no time to strike before we know what we're striking at. It's a time to ask serious questions of ourselves and our government and to not relax until we get the answers that we need.

My question is, *How will we respond?* I hope it's going to be in a positive way. I hope that Eastern does. First and foremost, I think that this college is called not so much to wipe out the terrorists as it is to eliminate the causes of terrorism. Let's be frank, direct, and honest at this point. Five thousand people die in one day because of the insanity of terrorists. It's shocking. I'm not going to get over it ever; I know that. But hear me: while we slept last night thirty thousand children under the age of twelve died of starvation or diseases related to malnutrition. Did you hear me? Five thousand die in Washington and in New York because of terrorists, but thirty thousand children die because of hunger.

There's a crucifix in front of an Episcopal church on Locust Street in downtown Philadelphia. One day as I was waiting for someone to pick me up on the corner I happened to look at the cross. There was a Bible verse from Lamentations underneath it. There on the cross was Jesus, and the verse beneath it read, "Does it mean nothing to you, O ye who pass by?" We should be outraged at five thousand people who innocently are put to death, but why are we not outraged by thirty thousand children who die every day? Does it mean nothing to you, O ye who pass by?

When I was in Haiti, I was at this restaurant table, ready to eat my meal. I looked to my right and there were three boys, naked almost. Dirty and filthy, with swelled bellies and hair turned rust-colored from malnutrition, the boys pressed their noses against the glass, staring at the food on my plate. The waiter, seeing my discomfort, moved in quickly and pulled down the shade and then he said to me, "Don't let them bother you; enjoy your meal." As if I could. But isn't that what we all do? Don't we all pull down the shade?

The president is absolutely right when he says the rest of the world is jealous of us, our freedoms, the wonderful life that we live. But the world is also resentful that we are 7 percent of the world's population and consume 42 percent of the world's resources. I want this school to distinguish itself in the time of this crisis with a new commitment. Let's commit ourselves to doing something about the hungry of the world. I want young men and young women to commit themselves to missionary enterprises that will alleviate these things. Rise up, O people of God; be done with lesser things. There are over two thousand verses of Scripture that call upon us to respond to the needs of the poor and the oppressed, the hungry, the downtrodden.

You ask, "What can we do?" I love this school because it has a vision. This year we moved downtown. We have this urban campus, and one of the programs there is to train people to start small businesses, economic development projects in Third World countries. This program started twelve years ago here at Eastern. In the early days we started feeding people into an organization called Opportunities International. This organization goes into Third World countries, goes into the slums, gathers people together who have no future. People in the slums of Manila, in the slums of Haiti. People in the barrios of Latin America. The organization teaches them how to create and run small businesses.

Now let me give you the results. (I did a fund-raising tour for them two months ago in Australia, and I had to get the statistics together.) In ten years, Opportunities International created two and a half million jobs. Did you hear that? This little school that some people write off as rinky-dink has fed into an organization that in turn has created two and a half million jobs. If there are six people to a family in a Third World country, you have to take that two and a half million people and multiply it by six to get how many people have been delivered from poverty, not for a day, not for a week, not for the year, but for the rest of their lives. For those of you who are business majors and economics majors, why would you want to go and work for General Motors or IBM when you can go to the poor and oppressed and do something that in eternity will have great value?

The whole thing got started, you know, because of a guy named Al Whitaker, multimillionaire who was the CEO of Bristol-Myers. One morning his wife looked across the table and asked, "Is this what you want to do with the rest of your life, Al? So what's it matter? President of a multinational corporation," she said, "all you're doing is spending your life making money for us and making rich people richer." That night at dinner he looked across the table and said, "The question you asked me so troubled me that I think you

should know, as I left the office today I resigned." That put
her down. "And we're going to commit ourselves to the poor
and oppressed." And that's where Opportunities
International came from.

Several years ago a friend of mine, Millard Fuller, said,
"Will you serve on my board?" He had this crazy idea that
they could build houses for poor people and get volunteers
to build them. I like Millard, so I said yes but didn't believe
in the vision. It's twenty-five years now. They have completed
one hundred thousand houses for poor people, and in the
next five years they will complete another one hundred
thousand. When the hurricane blew through Homestead,
Florida, many houses were blown down, save for the houses
that were built by the Habitat for Humanity people. When
the press asked Millard Fuller, "How do you explain this?"
He said, "Well, the first thing you have to understand is that
when Habitat builds a house it builds a house on the rock."
And these dumb reporters were going, "Yeah, Habitat builds
houses on rock." Of course, the real reason was that the people who built the houses were like the students at Eastern,
for I am here to say that the first college chapter of Habitat
for Humanity was organized at Eastern College. People who
build the houses don't know what they're doing, that's why
the houses lasted. No, that's true. If a beam needs five nails
here and five nails there, dumb Eastern students who don't
know what they're doing, they put twenty nails here, twenty
nails there. If you need this much cement, they put in *this*
much cement. Every one of the houses is overbuilt, and
when the winds come and the storms blow and beat upon
the houses, the houses stand because they are built on the
rock.

This is what we need to get into. This is how we respond.
We must not only build houses in America but also go to the
Third World, which is where Habitat began and started its
work, building houses for the poor in Haiti and the
Dominican Republic. One of my greatest regrets is that three

years ago I was invited by the foreign minister of Iraq—who, surprisingly, is an evangelical Christian—to come to Iraq and do evangelistic crusades. I had other commitments and I said no. I wish I could go back and cancel everything else and say, "I've got something more important to do." We have to commit ourselves to those who are being called our enemies.

I wish that half of the students here would say, "I'm going to Africa when I graduate. I'm going to work with those faith-based missionary organizations that are addressing the AIDS crisis because nobody else is." I just got back from Africa a month ago. The Evangelical Association for the Promotion of Education, the missionary organization that operates out of Heritage House, has started an AIDS hospice in Zimbabwe because there are thousands and thousands of children wandering the streets who have lost both mother and father, who have the HIV virus themselves, and who have no future.

If we are going to address terrorism we must get rid of the environment that breeds terrorism, an environment of suffering and despair.

Some contend that we cannot get rid of terrorism unless we deal with the Palestinian issue. The truth is, we evangelicals have been so anxious to make sure that the state of Israel survives that we have forgotten that Israel has been sending tanks into Arab territory, driving people off the land, leveling their houses, and building settlements in land that is not theirs. And we have never said a mumbling word. We are to be the voice for those who have no voice in America.

People ask why it happened, and there are all kinds of stupid explanations. I mean, nobody knows why it happened. There are two forces at work in the universe: the forces of darkness and the forces of light. The Zoroastrians believed they were equally balanced, and they weren't sure how the whole thing would turn out in the end. In the Hebrew tradition, there was hope that the forces of Yahweh, the forces of light would triumph over the forces of darkness, but it was a hope, it was only a hope.

But two thousand years ago something happened. The forces of light, the God of creation incarnated himself and then hung spread eagle to a Roman gibbet. At that hour, Satan and all the demonic forces of the universe conspired to destroy God. They thought they could do it. Please, Satan may be a lot of things, but Satan isn't stupid. Satan would not have rebelled against God had there not been a confidence on his part that he could win. He attacked God when God was in the form of weakness. When the day was over, the demonic forces must have been dancing. Satan must have been laughing. It looked as though they had gained control over the cosmos, that they were the rulers of the universe. But three days later Jesus staged a coup. "Up from the grave he arose, with a mighty triumph over his foes."

Oscar Cullmann, the great Swiss-German theologian, says we live between the times. He talked about D-day and V-day. He said that in every war there's a battle that decisively determines the outcome of the war. Civil War, Gettysburg. The Napoleonic wars, Waterloo. In World War II, it was D-day, the day in which the Allies landed on the beaches of Normandy; everybody knew that if the Allies were driven back to sea, it would be over for us. However, the Nazis knew that if a beachhead were established, it would be over for them. So much so that when we established the beachhead, Rommel joined the plot to assassinate Hitler because he knew that the Nazis could not win, and he knew that Hitler would never give up. The decisive battle was D-day, but let me point out to you that more people died in Europe between D-day and V-day than before D-day. Oh, the outcome of the war was never in doubt, but there was suffering, and there was death, and there was agony.

We live between God's D-day and God's V-day. The decisive battle has been fought and won in the death and resurrection of Jesus Christ. But the evil forces are still at work in the world, and that's why I call upon the Eastern students this morning to commit themselves to the cause of Christ to fight against the darkness. That's what we're about. If you are only interested in vocational education, then you diminish your dignity and cut into the mission of this school. We are called by God to be a people who join together to fight against the forces of darkness with what is an incredible weapon: love. Are you gonna do it?

One of these days Jesus is coming back. I don't know when. For that matter Jesus didn't know when, agreed? When they asked him, "When are you going to return and set up your kingdom?" He said, "I don't know, you're going to have to ask an American evangelist for the answer to that one."

But he is coming back. And between God's D-day and God's V-day, here's what it says in the first chapter of Philippians: that the one who has created the good work in us and through us will complete it (v. 6). That's what we are; we're the people to whom he does the good work he will complete on the day of his coming.

Seven

Deliver Us from Evil

Barbara Carlson
Unitarian Universalist Church
Bloomington, Indiana

> To Mercy, Pity, Peace, and Love
> All pray in their distress;
> And to these virtues of delight
> Return their thankfulness.
>
> For Mercy has a human heart,
> Pity, a human face,
> And Love, the human form divine,
> And Peace, the human dress.
>
> Then [everyone], of every clime,
> That prays in . . . distress,
> Prays to the human form divine,
> Love, Mercy, Pity, Peace.
> ("The Divine Image," William Blake)

Love, Mercy, Pity, Peace. Be with us now.
Mercy, Pity, Peace, Love. Deliver us from evil.
For this week we have known the Apocalypse.

Not some far-off dread event of disturbed imagination, but horror unfolding before our very eyes. A tragedy of unimaginable proportions in our beloved land.

Our innocence has been shaken before. Oklahoma City, a plane exploding over Scotland, another diving into the Atlantic, the bombing of our embassies in Kenya and Tanzania, the attempted sinking of the *U.S.S. Cole*—all terrorist acts tragic in their destruction and loss of life. Yet the magnitude of this past week's massacre, the killing and maiming of innocents—beloved friends, relatives, wives, husbands, sons, daughters, rescuers—has ripped us open. Innocent people have been sacrificed. There is no more innocence for us as a people and a nation.

We now know the terrible vulnerability that others in our world experience every day. Israeli and Palestinian people live in constant threat of terrorism, as do the people of Northern Ireland where those who call themselves Christian have been bent on destroying one another longer than I can remember.

How can we hold what we have seen and what we now know? How can we hold what we *do not know?* Our fear of the evil unseen that may yet be lurking, waiting to strike, perpetrated by imaginations crazed by hatred, grief, vengefulness, and God only knows.

How can we protect the innocent and all we love? Who will deliver us from evil?

It's easier, somehow, to say what won't deliver us. We know that violence will not deliver us from evil. The truth that violence begets more violence is a reality that can be grasped by an intelligent schoolchild.

We know that blaming and scapegoating a whole group or nation or religion for the sins of a few is a dangerous form of psychic violence. All Muslims are not our enemies. Many are our friends. Many are peace-loving people. Islam is not the enemy, nor does the Koran sanction this terrible tragedy anymore than the loving teachings of Jesus are responsible for the insanity in Northern Ireland.

Violence only destroys. It can never create. Only mercy (compassion), peace, and love will deliver us from evil. This is the message of all the great religions and all the peacemakers of all times.

Another universal truth was expressed by the great Native American chief Black Elk. Black Elk stood on a high mountain, and gazing out, he saw that the sacred hoop of his people was one of "many hoops that made one circle, wide as daylight and as starlight . . . , to shelter all the children of one mother and one father." And he "saw that it was holy."

One mother, one father, one human family.

In our own time Dr. Martin Luther King Jr. was totally converted to the philosophy and practice of nonviolence after a bombing attack on his own home and family. King embraced what Father Dan Berrigan has called an *Ethic of Resurrection:* the commitment to act affirmatively for life in the presence of death.

The commitment to act affirmatively for life can deliver us from evil.

The commitment to minister to a wounded world begins (but does not end) with ministering to ourselves.

Be gentle with yourselves, dear people. We are all in grief. At least one among us has lost a friend. [A member's] friend was on the plane that hit the Pentagon.

We are glad for all who are home safe, yet we are all diminished by the horror of this past week. We need to acknowledge that. Some have told me of sleepless nights, difficulty in concentrating, and anxiety and fear for the safety of children and loved ones. Beloved, these are normal reactions to an incredibly abnormal situation.

The human psyche can only absorb so much at one time. Each of us has our own way and pace of dealing with what has happened. I can't think of an encounter I've had this past week—in the church, in my neighborhood, or in the larger community—where this trauma has not been part of the conversation. I know I need to talk about it. I need reality checks.

And we need to be gentle with those whose needs are different from our own. Some need to carry on business as usual. One friend said that if she didn't carry on her normal functions and duties, she felt she would be granting another victory to terrorists. Another friend knew she needed to take some time out and just be with her family. Both are to be honored as ways people are seeking to cope with shock and grief in the aftermath of tragedy. Let us be gentle with each other and with ourselves.

Take time for what sustains you and connects you affirmatively with life. Connect with your religious community, as you are doing here today.

In addition to the service on Tuesday evening, our sanctuary was open each day this past week, and several came in to meditate and pray. Our sanctuary will be open in the week to come. Participation in a community of caring and service to others is important. The most important part of our security is each other. We need to look out for each other, and we need to work together.

I received a message from Matthew Fox, the founder and director of the University of Creation Spirituality. He said the events of this past week are a perversion of creativity—the demonic is the other side of divine creativity. He regretted that our intelligence was not creative enough to thwart them. And he added: "One lesson I derived from our Iroquois elders in our prayer circle Tuesday was the teaching not to wallow in the media prolongation of this story of evil, but to get on with living and working to prevent it in the future and to heal its deep wounds."

In closing, let us pray for our president, our leaders, and for the leaders of all nations that they may be guided in wisdom to decisions and right action for the healing of our country and our world.

Leaders like Lee Hamilton of Indiana and former president Jimmy Carter are among those who emphasize the need for a global commitment to end terrorism without retaliatory strikes that destroy the innocent and miss an elusive foe.

Even in these terrible days, may we and our leaders be delivered from the evil of smug righteousness as we remember the actions of our own country that have brought suffering in many places.

As we sing our closing song all who wish are invited to come forward and light a candle.

Some of us may not be in agreement on the ways to peace, but all of us are in agreement on the goal, so let this light be your own personal prayer and your commitment to act in some way for peace this week—by a prayer, a letter to the president, reaching out to Muslim friends, some action of your own choosing. "Let there be peace on earth, and let it begin with me."

Eight

Will Life Ever Be the Same Again? Reflections on John 2

Tim Dearborn
Seattle Pacific University
Opening Communion Service

Like anxious relatives in an ER waiting room, we've huddled together this past week around our TVs, over prolonged long-distance phone conversations, through gathering in historic numbers at churches, and in throngs filling spontaneous memorials with candles and flowers. "Any news? What have you heard? Is it really that bad? What's going to happen next?" Everything else in our lives stopped. All else seemed trivial, insignificant, not as important as we'd previously thought.

The horrific images of planes piercing buildings, a sight that surpassed our most hideous nightmares, have been replayed over and over. Such evil and destruction! Such death! Nearly six thousand people died on September 11, 2001. Also dying was our confidence in false forms of security, the illusion of our invincibility, possibly some of the protective aura generated by our role as a superpower. These crumbled along with the buildings and planes, brought down by $2 box knives. One *New York Times* journalist describes the morning of September 11 as the last day of the old world.

We've heard the plaintive lament aired on network news: "Why, God? Where are you? Why did you allow such evil to destroy such innocence?" This cry has echoed our own dismay, reverberating over and over again through our souls.

Yet, equaling the tears we've wept in grief and anger, have been the tears provoked by countless images of heroism and human kindness. The greatness of the human spirit expressed by way of cell phone in the words of a thirty-one-year-old wife to her hostage husband: "Yes, honey, I agree. You have to try to stop the hijackers. I love you. Good-bye." Three hundred firefighters running the wrong way up the stairs, laying down their lives for total strangers. None of us will ever look at firefighters the same again. The overwhelming outpouring of kindness and concern, food, hands, money, prayers! Networks broadcasting nonstop news for days, without a single ad, refusing to defile our national grief with commercials.

The greatness of the human spirit; America at its best!

Now we begin asking, When will life return to normal? Will it? Ever? A lot has changed since Tuesday. Not simply our sense of security, not only the arrogance of our power, nor our illusion of being insulated from the rest of the world. I hope something far deeper. As one pastor preached on Sunday the 16th: "Whether or not the nation changes for the better in the days ahead will depend on our ability to see ourselves as a nation not only under attack but also under God."

French philosopher Paul Ricoeur describes these emergency-room moments in our lives as "limit experiences"—an experience that pushes us beyond the limits of imaginable, normal life. Worse than we could imagine, we think that on the other side of that experience is only emptiness, nothingness, loss. But Ricoeur calls us to remember that such is not the case. Beyond the limit there is more; there is God, whose love knows no limit. Evil does not have the last word. Beyond the limits of evil's horror is the wondrous God's incarnate, crucified, resurrected Word giving us new life.

Months ago I selected this text and title for today. For reasons not imagined then, I think they're still appropriate. The text describes John's account of Jesus' first miracle and his first public action. One seemed capriciously frivolous—turning water into wine to keep a wedding party going. The other was violently scandalous—the Prince of Peace whipping religious merchants out of the Temple. At stake was more than a wedding host saving face, more than merchants making money from others' devotion. For the One who was the Lord and Maker of water to transform it into wine should not surprise us. For the One whose own flesh is the temple—the place of encounter between humanity and divinity—to decry defiling the earthly temple with efforts to buy God's favor with paltry trinkets of devotion is no surprise either. However, what is surprising is our Lord's shadowy comments that surround his actions: "My [time] has not yet come." "Destroy this temple, and in three days I will raise it up."

Jesus is obviously alluding to the greatest catastrophe of history—not Tuesday, September 11, 2001, but Good Friday, when we crucified the Son of God. Jesus was referring to the table around which we celebrate today. Like the wedding at Cana, this wine is also that of a wedding, the foretaste of our marriage as the bride of Christ. The cross—the temple of Christ brought down in death—was the ultimate push by humanity beyond the limit; but God pushed beyond that—weaving it into his redemptive purposes, carrying Christ's death into the resurrection. Jesus defeated death so that we may experience life beyond our limits—rising with him into new life. In the fourth century, Athanasius wrote: "Disciples of Christ despise death; they take the offensive against it and, instead of fearing it, by the sign of the cross and by faith in Christ trample on it as on something dead. . . . Death is no longer terrible"(*de Incarnatione:* 57). It's no wonder that during last Friday's Day of Mourning Services at the National Cathedral in Washington D.C., the cameras seemed irresistibly drawn to the crucifix hanging over the high altar, rotating between the assembly of all our nation's recent presidents, and the images of the cross. Presidential power bowing before the crucified King of creation. Inescapably, undeniably, this is the only answer to the "Why, God? Where are you, God?" questions.

So what will we do? If this is the end of the old world and the beginning of a new one, what kind will it be? A world of fear and fortresses? As Augustine reminds us in the *City of God,* there are only two kinds of cities, and can we say, two kinds of people and nations: the city of self-love and the city of God's love. Maybe we've danced too long with self-love, living for ourselves, preoccupied with protecting our personal and national interests, grabbing what little we could while we could.

America is great, the human spirit expresses greatness, when it lives in that other city. Seeking greater paths of service rather than whining over others getting more of the pie than we do. Fearlessly trampling on death rather than fleeing when life is tough. Stewarding all with which the Lord of the earth and of history has entrusted us not simply for ourselves but for the sake of all the earth and history. This is a history-shaping moment. We are writing the first chapters not of a new millennium, but some would say of a new world. Augustine warns us that the two cities exist side by side. They overlap within even our own hearts. The good news is that the city motivated by greed, fear, and conceit eventually collapses in the self-absorption of its own egotism. Christ died to lead us out of our captivity to that city. We are raised with him into the city of God's love. Every empire that has prided itself on itself has died, unable to withstand assaults from the inside and out. Only the city of God, founded on the cross of Christ and motivated by the love of God, endures. May we reflect citizenship in that city, the kingdom of God!

What kind of nation, what kind of people, what kind of campus will we be? This is a time for the kind of patriotism defined by Simone Weil as a "tender affection for one's country, ever seeking that which is its best." It's time also for something far greater. To come out of our captivity to the city of self-love, to abandon our despair, to trample on our terrors and fears, and to follow Jesus, ever willing to lay down our lives en route to the future filled with unshakable hope. Those whom we call heroes today didn't wake up heroes last Tuesday morning, the 11th. In the impulse of the moment their greatness was called forth, for no greater love has anyone than those who lay down their life for another. Not taking their own lives by seeking to take down as many others as possible, but sacrificing their lives, seeking to save as many as they could.

Mary's first impulse when confronted with a need, even a relatively trivial one, was complete trust: "[Listen to my son.] Do whatever he tells you" (John 2:5). May God's Spirit enable that to be the impulse of our lives. Jesus whipped away all effort to buy our way into God's favor. He cleared the court of the Gentiles, the only place where people from all nations, those outside the fold of acceptability, non-Jews, could worship the Lord. May God cleanse the temples of our souls. May God cleanse our campus and nation, that we might be a community where all people are embraced in Christ—meriting that embrace simply because of Christ, a community whose first and only impulse is complete trust in the Lord. There will be no peace in the world until we live with mutual understanding rather than prejudice, seek justice for all people, and pursue as our ultimate loyalty life in the kingdom of the reconciling God. "Listen to my Son. Do whatever he tells you."

Nine

Your Glory, O Israel, Lies Slain on the High Places

Nancy A. De Vries
The Colgate University Church

(2 Samuel 1:1-27; Psalm 55; Luke 1:68-79)

Stunning and powerful are the stories, the historical accounts in the Old Testament of the battles of ancient Israel and Judah, of Saul and Jonathan, of David, of the kings and the tribes. These stories have their own magnificent truth. They are overflowing with passion and violence. They are full of courage, determination; full of cataclysmic grief. For many of us, if we know these stories and these passages, most, if not all, of our lives they have seemed far away. They seemed to belong to an ancient time when deaths of hundreds and thousands of people all at once seemed somehow normal, and totally other than our own experience.

Now these stories belong to us. They are ours in a way that even last Sunday they were not. They are ours, whether we are Americans, or America is our host country, or we are somewhere in between. For thousands of us have died. Americans and Zimbabweans, Anglo-Saxons, and Afro-Caribbeans; those who love this country, and those who are not so sure; those who have ties to another country, and

71

those who have been here for multiple generations. Now we are one people; this tragedy has made us one.

We must go into this time and acknowledge it; it is our own. Like the psalmist, we may be so overcome that we wish to go back in time, to escape.

> My heart is in anguish within me,
>   the terrors of death have fallen upon me.
> Fear and trembling come upon me,
>   and horror overwhelms me.
> And I say, "O that I had wings like a dove!
>   I would fly away and be at rest;
> truly, I would flee far away;
>   I would lodge in the wilderness;
> I would hurry to find a shelter for myself
>   from the raging wind and tempest." (Psalm 55:4-8)

And we must get on with our lives; we must. But we must also be honest and acknowledge that there is no getting on with the lives that we lived until Tuesday morning.

There are things that change us forever, and make us and our lives forever changed: things as personal and seemingly private as taking a lover; or events in no way simple, such as sustaining a death. There are many times such as these. There are definitive experiences after which life cannot be the same as it was before; and we are forever changed.

Now we stand at such a juncture. We in the United States frequently think of how things have an impact on us as individuals. Now, whether we wish it for ourselves or not, we will learn how this event shall have an impact on us as a nation.

> Your glory, O Israel, lies slain
>   upon your high places!
> How the mighty have fallen! (2 Samuel 1:19)

We who are Christian, who are people of faith, have both responsibility and opportunity for this moment. Let us ask ourselves, what does it mean to be people of faith at such a moment? What does it mean to follow after the one who gave himself over to death so that we know beyond a doubt that we have a God who suffers with us? What does it mean that we call our God, "Lord of the Nations?" What does it mean that we affirm the oneness of the body of Christ? What does it mean for us now that we say that God is at the first and the last, the God of love? What does it mean that we say God is a God who wills for us peace and not war, life and not death, and that God is a God of all consolation?

There are many things it means for us to believe and affirm these things, and to have the mind and heart of Jesus Christ. And this nation and the world need our voices. A future needs now to be built, my brothers and sisters in Christ. It must be a future for all men and women, for all boys and girls. Children must not become parentless in Teaneck or in Ramallah. Innocent people must not die on Canal Street or in the cafes of Tel Aviv. As sons and daughters of God, and as those who follow after the Lord of Life and the Prince of Peace, we must build a future that ensures justice for all, plenty and not want, freedom from violence for all the peoples and nations of this world. These things are not easily built, but to do so is our calling.

We must learn from the suffering of our own people in so many ways. We must learn to be wise as serpents and gentle as doves. We must learn today the things that make for peace, and some of those things will be hard lessons for all of us, whether we tend toward military might or nonviolence as a response. We must bind one another up as a nation. We must be strong. We must be compassionate. We must find credible and genuine ways to be both of these at the same time.

Always remember, my brothers and sisters in faith, that God creates the future. The Lord of the Universe calls us into it and accompanies us there. There is a future for our entire world as well as our country that we must create. It is a future characterized by the goodness and greatness of God. It is a future that is secure. It is a future into which we may move, confidently, without all the answers, but always with God.

Near the end of the first century, when Christians were in fear for their lives, and Nero was using Christians as human torches at garden parties, there was a magnificent vision of a future with peace for all people, a new heaven and a new earth, that is represented in these powerful, beautiful words:

> Then I saw a new heaven and a new earth; for the first heaven and the first earth had passed away, and the sea was no more. And I saw the holy city, the new Jerusalem, coming down out of heaven from God, prepared as a bride adorned for her husband. And I heard a loud voice from the throne saying,
>> "See, the home of God is among mortals.
>> He will dwell with them;
>> they will be his peoples,
>> and God himself will be with them;
>> he will wipe every tear from their eyes.
>> Death will be no more;
>> mourning and crying and pain will be no more,
>> for the first things have passed away."
> And the one who was seated on the throne said, "See, I am making all things new." (Revelation 21:1-5)

Let us remember that this is the future to which we are called as architects and builders. And let us say with Zechariah:

> "Blessed be the Lord God . . . ,
>> for he has looked favorably on his people and redeemed them.
> He has raised up a mighty savior for us
>> in the house of his servant David,
> as he spoke through the mouth of his holy prophets from of old,
>> that we would be saved from our enemies and from the hand of all who hate us.

Thus he has shown the mercy promised to our ancestors,
    and has remembered his holy covenant,
the oath that he swore to our ancestor Abraham,
    to grant us that we, being rescued from the hands of our
        enemies,
might serve him without fear, in holiness and righteousness
    before him all our days.
By the tender mercy of our God,
    the dawn from on high will break upon us,
    to give light to those who sit in darkness and in the shad-
      ow of death,
    to guide our feet into the way of peace."
(Luke 1:68-75, 78-79)

Let us pray.

Ten

Power to Rise Again

S. Renee Franklin*
Tuskegee University

(Psalm 79:1-9; Jeremiah 8:18–9:1; Luke 16:1-13)

Most, if not all, of us have experienced some degree of loss, hurt, grief; and certainly people all over our nation and world—especially those who lost loved ones during the tragic events of September 11—are among those with whom we most empathize in this regard.

Just as we struggle with suffering on a personal level, facing the devastation such as we have seen and are experiencing today raises questions in our minds, questions that we are uncertain have hope-filled answers: *Why did this happen to me/us? The pain is so deep, when will healing come? Why did God do this/allow this to happen? When will all of this violence end? Why must the suffering and pain last so long? Where is God? Is there really a God? How will we get through this? Will we ever have joy, peace, and security again?* We wonder if we can ever rise above our circumstances. Through our personal and

---
*The Reverend S. Renee Franklin is Campus Minister for the Wesley Foundation United Methodist Campus Ministry at Tennessee State University.

communal pain we begin to identify with the voice that cries out in Jeremiah 8:22: "Is there no balm in Gilead?"

Jeremiah lamented for Judah because of their suffering and pain. It had become so horrific. Although he had continually served as God's voice calling them to repentance, and could see and had prophesied to them about their impending demise, his heart was heavy, and his message speaks of hopelessness for the people. He/they needed to know that God had not abandoned them and that there was still some hope for their deliverance and recovery. This sounds so familiar as we look at our present situation here in America. Surely we don't want to continue to replay the scenes of destruction and devastation, which have been aired on television constantly since the tragedy. Yet, a little more than a week later, and months and years to come, many will continue to cry out in so many words, Is there no balm in Gilead?

Like in personal circumstances, it is difficult for us to let go or forget about experiences that have brought us much grief and pain. The pictures of the incidents remain fresh in our minds, and we often find ourselves crying and having nightmares because we have difficulty overcoming our grief. However, we know and have at times experienced that the time must come when we have to move on. We can't stay where we are—oft times dwelling in the tombs of grief or wallowing in self-pity. To do so provides no hope for us or anyone else. But, as we cry out to God for healing and hope, God guides us, strengthens us, and empowers us to contribute to our own healing as instruments enabling *all things*—even in these difficult circumstances—to *work together for good.*

While the cry of Jeremiah appears to ring of little or no hope, we know the story doesn't end there. For eventually, some years later, God does enter into a new covenant relationship with Judah. Deliverance does come. However, deliverance does not necessarily come at the wave of a magic

77

wand. While God is able to perform miracles beyond our ability to understand, God often requires some activity on our part to play a role in bringing it to pass.

In the case of the people of Israel, they needed to repent of their sins and turn away from worshiping other gods, and serve God only. Even though suffering, pain, and devastation is not always a result of something you or I have done wrong, God still can use us as instruments through whom deliverance is brought to bear.

Let's look at it on a personal level. Numerous biblical accounts tell of persons who had infirmities who turned to the Lord for healing and deliverance. In many situations, there was something they were called to do as a part of the healing process. Naaman, the commander who had leprosy, was told by the prophet to wash in the Jordan River seven times before he experienced his healing. The man born blind, for whom Jesus formed clay and put it on his eyes, was instructed to go to a pool and wash his eyes. It was only after that that he received sight. Even beyond the biblical era, there were those such as Booker T. Washington, Mother Teresa, numerous civil rights leaders, and many others who, as people of faith, served as instruments of deliverance and hope for themselves and others.

God certainly cares about our hurts, pains, and struggles. God is not silent. God is not absent. Even though God does not always prevent us from having to experience difficult circumstances, God has not left us alone, and will see us through if we would turn to God.

The Luke text for today's lectionary initially seemed to me to be out of place alongside that from Jeremiah. Yet I found that it also brings some light to how we can gain healing and deliverance—and rise above our circumstances. In this text, we find Jesus sharing with his disciples, as was often the case. On the heels of such parables as the lost coin and the prodigal son, Jesus tells the disciples a story of a shrewd businessman. This man failed to be faithful in managing the financial affairs of his boss. He was called to task on it and told that he would lose his job as a result. The businessman or manager, as Jesus describes him, could have easily folded his hands and given up, feeling that he could probably never get another decent job. Rather, he immediately got busy contacting those who owed his boss, and worked out a deal with them to ensure the debts were paid to some degree, and to create new opportunities for him to rebuild. His boss commended him. As well, Jesus praised his shrewdness, for the manager did not dwell on his unfortunate circumstance, but readily began to make steps to rise above it.

Certainly, it is natural for us to struggle to get through the grief and pain of our losses. However, with God's help, we can rise again. Rise above our circumstances and create new opportunities for healing and growth. Much of this is taking place as we see the many people assisting with the recovery and cleanup in New York City. It is evident when we see thousands of people donating blood all over the country. Some people don't know where they are getting the strength to continue, and yet work twelve- and fourteen-hour days to help with the process of healing and rebuilding lives. I am convinced that God is present; as God can make a way out of no way. People of faith are finding strength and courage to rise above it all. They are finding the power to rise again.

A clergy friend of mine told a story recently of how he frequently visits New York City for business meetings. Whenever he's there, a friend of his is always inviting him to some cultural event to help him get some culture, being the Southerner that he is. On one particular visit, she took him to an art gallery for an exhibit. While there, she became engaged in a lengthy conversation with the gallery owner, which left my friend to browse around looking at the exhibit. Concerned that what he saw didn't appear to be the "real" exhibit, my friend interrupted the conversation and asked where the exhibit was. To his surprise, she said,

"You're looking at it." The exhibit was of graffiti. She explained that a wealthy New Yorker paid several artists to develop paintings around obscenities found in graffiti. While the graffiti was clearly visible, the artists painted beautiful colors and shapes, which transformed the original appearance from ugly and profane to an expression of beauty. My friend shared this story to remind us that we may see massive ugliness, profanity, and destruction, but the paintbrush is in our hands. We are called to take what we see—whatever we have experienced—and transform it into something new. With God's help, we have the power not only to change our personal situations, but to change the world.

In the midst of anger, hatred, and constant threat of warfare, God calls us to be instruments of love, peace, reconciliation, and hope. Despite all of the players among the leaders of our nation and world, God still calls *us* to make a difference. Certainly we must remain prayerful—not only asking God to help, protect, and bless us, but also, in prayer, listening for God's counsel. God can and will guide us to make the right decisions to bring deliverance. Sometimes we may feel like a lone voice, but so was Jeremiah.

Congresswoman Barbara Lee, to me, appears to be a lone voice crying out for caution and care before we lead to further destruction at home and abroad. She cast the lone vote against giving President Bush free rein on decisions regarding our country engaging in warfare. She has been rejected by colleagues, threatened, and ridiculed by many because of the stand she has taken. Although our nation is ready to use physical warfare as a means for us to rise again, I am convinced that if we are not called and led by God into this war, we will never rise again. With God we have the power to rise again. With God we can make the appropriate moves and necessary sacrifices to participate in our healing and deliverance. With God leading us, guiding us, empowering us, we can overcome any obstacle or situation in life. Whether it is a personal struggle with physical illness or the difficulty of confronting terrorists in the world, God gives us the power to rise again.

Jesus is our ultimate example of what it means to rise again, not only with his resurrection from the grave but also through his living presence in each of our lives. He exercised power over sin and death and gives us power to live as children of God in a world where there is so much death and destruction. We don't have to wait until the resurrection of all of the saints to rise again. Each time we allow God to use us as instruments of healing and deliverance in the lives of individuals as well as in the world as a whole, Christ rises within the world and us.

The Scriptures empower us to rise above our circumstances. The Holy Spirit empowers us to rise above our circumstances. As well, the songs of Zion remind us that we have the power to rise again. Jeremiah cried out, and many today join him, voicing the sentiment: "Is there no balm in Gilead? Is there no physician there? Why then has the health of my poor people not been restored?" (Jeremiah 8:22). But with faith, hope, and the power of God leading us, we can join our ancestors who were overcomers and who possessed the power to rise again. We, like them, can respond:

There is a balm in Gilead to make the wounded whole;
There is a balm in Gilead to heal the sin-sick soul.

Sometimes I feel discouraged, and think my work's in vain,
But then the Holy Spirit revives my soul again.

There is a balm in Gilead to make the wounded whole;
There is a balm in Gilead to heal the sin-sick soul.

(So) Don't (you) ever feel discouraged, for Jesus is your friend,
And if you look for knowledge, he'll ne'er refuse to lend.

There is a balm in Gilead to make the wounded whole;
There is a balm in Gilead to heal the sin-sick soul.

(African American spiritual)

The word of God for the people of God. Thanks be to God.

Eleven

Twenty-fourth Sunday in Ordinary Time

Thomas E. Gaughan
The Basilica of the Sacred Heart
University of Notre Dame

(Exodus 32:7-11, 13-14; Luke 15:1-32; 1 Timothy 1:12-17)

September 11, 2001. A date that we have forever etched into our hearts and minds, and another date of infamy for history to record. But we who live through this dark chapter struggle. We struggle to make sense of it all. We struggle to articulate our feelings and sentiments. We struggle to discern paths to follow. But in these struggles we must remind ourselves that we do not walk through life alone. We have the brilliance of grace shining through God's Word to be our comfort and our direction.

How can we comprehend the terror and anguish of this past week? The pain inflicted upon us has been so great that we could easily allow fear to numb our hearts, and vengeful rage to blind us from the things we *know* to be true. Yet at the very cornerstone of our faith we know that death has no victory. Death does not have the final word.

These are difficult words to hold on to in the face of such unbearable pain and sorrow and death. But we must grasp this cornerstone as ours, as we live through this painful reality and move into an uncertain future.

In the face of such incomprehensible horror and massive infliction of pain and death, we could easily recoil, overwhelmed, into hopelessness, despair, and anger. But our gospel teaches us an unshakable truth, the rock solid foundation of our lives. God's love is greater than our reasoning, broader than our wildest imagination, and deeper than our most heinous capacity for sin.

The three parables in today's gospel illustrate for us a love that defies all reasoning. For *no* good shepherd would leave his sheep. No one so poor as to need to search out and find a tiny lost coin could ever celebrate a feast over its recovery. And the *father* in the final parable acts in a prodigal way, even an insane way. He gave away property the son had *no* claim to and then welcomed him home again as a son.

None of us would typically behave in these ways. But there you have the love of God. All three parables, from the human perspective and reason, make no sense. But *all* demonstrate a love beyond our capacity to reason; far higher than *our* sense of justice; deeper and more embracing than we could ever hope for, with its capacity to heal, reconcile, and forgive.

This, our gospel of love, shines on us as a beacon of hope, strength, and guidance in one of the darkest chapters of American history. In this gospel light, let us remember that in the face of hatred we must *not*, as individuals and as a nation, succumb to the temptation to allow revenge to rule us.

An evil has pierced our land. It seeks to destroy our way of life, lives, our souls and spirit. But we must *not* let the veins of such an evil penetrate our hearts. For if we disregard the gospel of love and simply match pain for pain in a spirit of revenge, then evil will have certainly accomplished its goal.

As a people of faith, in the face of the devastation of this past week, we stand, like the disciples crushed by the devastation of the crucifixion. But unlike the disciples, *we* need *not* scatter in fear and confusion because we *know* what the disciples would soon learn: that we find our hope in the victorious triumph of the cross.

We know and believe to be true that the power*ful* embrace of God's transformative, life-giving love rendered powerless the powers of evil demonstrated in the crucifixion. We live a real faith and we know that death has no power to quench life's spirit; sin has no power to weaken love.

And we, as a people, have held to that truth. For love, indeed, has been the response of millions who have gathered to pray, who have given blood, and who have donated money in the relief effort. Love has most certainly been the response of those who have risked and who continue to risk their lives in the search for survivors and the recovery of the dead.

In light of all of the events of this past week, we must accept the deeper challenge of the gospel: to allow this unfathomable love of God to so permeate our being that our response to these attacks becomes not only compassion for our own, but prayers of forgiveness for our enemies.

We stand on the brink of our national defense's response to seek justice for the attacks of this past Tuesday. United with other nations, we seek to rid the world of terrorist activity. Surely, it would seem, we are on the brink of war.

We will find pain, suffering, trials, and hardships in the unforeseeable future. And so we must pray faithfully and diligently, for ourselves, our nation, and our world. And we must be steadfast in our prayers, so that through it all, as individuals and as a nation, we keep our gospel truths before us. They will focus and guide us so that our labors might result in a world of lasting peace.

These times will test our faith in the fiery furnace of human sinfulness. Let us pray for ourselves and our country, that the love of God, which our gospel celebrates, will reign in our hearts. May God deliver us from the contamination of hatred and revenge and lead us to seek a justice that will lead us to peace.

And let us pray, too, for the ongoing conversion of our hearts and the hearts of all people so that we might one day live together free from fear, as true and loving children of God.

Amen.

Twelve

Outer Turmoil, Inner Strength

Peter J. Gomes
Memorial Church, Harvard University

> Set thy heart aright, and constantly endure, and make not
> haste in time of calamity. (Ecclesiasticus 2:2 KJV)

Let me begin with an observation, one might say, of comparative religion. I understand that in the traditions and liturgies of the Greek Orthodox Church, our brethren in the East, that when a child is baptized—and by "child" I mean an infant, not a squalling seven-year-old, but a real infant, literally still damp—after the baptism has been performed, the minister or priest or bishop takes his very large pectoral cross—twice the size of mine—and forcefully strikes the little child on its breast, so hard that it leaves a mark, and so hard that it hurts the child, and the child screams.

In the West, we give the child roses. What is the difference here?

The symbolism of the Eastern baptism is clear, indicating that the child who has been baptized into Christ must bear the cross, and that the cross is a sign not of ease or of victory or of prosperity or of success, but of sorrow, suffering, pain, and death; and by it those things are overcome. It is important to remember that. The symbol of our Christian faith is this very cross that you see on that holy table, carved in that choir screen, worn around the necks of many of us, and held in honor and esteemed by all of us; and it stands to remind us of the troubles of the world that placed our Savior upon it for sins that he did not commit. We Christians, therefore, like those Greek Orthodox babies, ought to expect trouble, turmoil, and tribulation as the normal course of life. We don't, however; and we have been seduced by a false and phony version of the Christian faith which suggests that by our faith we are immune to trouble.

Because we have been nice to God, our thinking goes, then God should be nice to us. Because you have interrupted your normal routine and come here today, God should somehow take note of it, mark it down in the book, and spare you any trouble, tribulation, turmoil, or difficulty. Tribulation, we know, happens only to bad people: should it therefore be happening in spades to all those people in Canaday Hall as I speak, those who are not here this morning but are just getting up out of bed, recovering from a night of pleasure and satiety? Tribulation happens only to the nonobservant and the bad people; and when, as Rabbi Kushner so famously and quite profitably noted, bad things happen to good people, we feel that something has gone terribly wrong. God is not supposed to behave that way, we think, for that is not part of the deal; and we ask, "Where is God?" I'll get back to that question, but that is what we ask.

Now, let me hasten to say that the answer to that conundrum is not a false conception of God. The issue has nothing whatsoever to do with the so-called "death of God," and everything to do with the life and the faith of the believer. It is not the death of God that should concern us; it is the questionable state of the life of the believer. God does not spare us from turmoil, which even the most casual observance of the Scriptures tells us; God strengthens us for turmoil, and we can find that in the Good Book as well. It is a shabby faith that suggests that God is to do all the heavy lifting and that you and I are to do none. The whole record of Scripture, from Genesis to Revelation, and the whole experience of the people of God from Good Friday down to and beyond Tuesday, September 11, suggest that faith is forged on the anvil of human adversity. No adversity; no faith.

Consider the lessons we heard this morning. In the first lesson, from one of the ancient books of the Jews, the book of Ecclesiasticus in the Apocrypha, could it be put any plainer? "My son, if thou comest to serve the Lord, prepare thy soul for temptation. Set thy heart aright, and constantly endure, and do not make haste in time of calamity" (2:1-2). You don't need a degree in Hebrew Bible or exegesis to figure out what that is saying. What is the context for these words? Trouble, turmoil, tribulation, and temptation: that's the given, that's the context. What is the response for calamity? Endurance. Don't rush, don't panic. What are we to do in calamitous times? We are to slow down. We are to inquire. We are to endure. Tribulation does not invite haste; it invites contemplation, reflection, perseverance, and endurance.

Where may we turn for examples of what I am trying to say that the Scriptures say to us? We, with our Jewish brethren, are in the middle of the great "Days of Awe," with the beginning of the New Year and the Day of Atonement; and when the Jewish people celebrate these Days of Awe and begin their new year and atone for their sins, they always remember two things. First, they remember the troubles and the tribulations through which they have been, and they recite the history, not of their victories, but of their sorrows and their troubles. They remind themselves and one another, and everybody else, of how they have been formed and forged through the experience of trial and tribulation. They remember those things.

The second thing they remember is how the Lord delivered them out of those troubles and helped them to endure and bear and eventually overcome them. They are reminded of that, and they remind themselves of it over and over and over again; and when it is said that "it is not the Jew who keeps the law, but the law which keeps the Jew," it is to this process of remembrance, endurance, and deliverance that the aphorism speaks.

Again, it says in the book of Ecclesiasticus, "Look at the generations of old, and see. Whoever did put his trust in the Lord, and was ashamed? Or who did abide in his fear, and was forsaken? Or who did call upon him, and he despised him?" (2:10). The history of the Jews in the world is not a history of escape from trouble: would that it were, but it is not. It is the record of endurance through tribulation, an endurance which would have been impossible without God. If any people had the right to claim that "God was dead," or at least on sabbatical, it was the Jews; but they never have said it, and they never will, for they know better. They do not worship a metaphor or a simile, or a theological construct. They worship the One who stands beside them and who has been with them from Egypt to Auschwitz and beyond, and who enables them to stand up to all that a world of tribulation can throw at them. If we want to know about outer turmoil and inner strength, we need look no further than to our neighbors the Jews. Remember, they wrote the book on the subject.

We may also look a little closer to home. We may look to the authentic witness of the Christian faith to which we bear, in this church, unambiguous allegiance. We do not just believe in God in general or in a spiritual hope; we believe in Jesus Christ, who is all that we can fully know about God. So, we look at this tradition for inner strength in the midst of outer turmoil.

Consider Saint Paul, a Jew and a Christian, and consider his view of things in a less than agreeable world. I hope you heard that second lesson read this morning in J. B. Phillips's pungent prose; I chose it so it would get your attention.

Listen to what Saint Paul says: "We are handicapped on all sides"—a very fashionable translation of the word, but apt— "but we are never frustrated; we are puzzled, but never in despair. We are persecuted, but we never have to stand it alone, [and . . .]"—this fourth part is the part I like the most—"we may be knocked down but we are never knocked out!" (2 Corinthians 4:8-9).

Now Paul is not an abstract theologian, like so many of my colleagues: Paul speaks from the experience of a frustrated but not defeated believer. This is not the sort of "How to Be Leaders and Win" sort of stuff that he writes; this is not the kind of CEO book that they trot out in the business school and in motivational seminars. No. Paul writes out of failure, frustration, and conflict but never out of despair. If you are looking for something to read in these troublesome times, do not turn to books of cheap inspiration and handy-dandy aphorisms; do not look for feel-good and no-stress and a lot-of-gain-and-no-pain kinds of books. They're all out there, and you will be sorely tempted; but if you want to read something useful during these times, my brothers and sisters in Christ, read the letters of Paul. Read them and weep! Read them and rejoice! Read them and understand that neither you nor I are the first people in the world ever to face sorrow, death, frustration, or terror. We are not the first, and there is a record of coping here that is not merely of coping but of overcoming. If you do not wish to succumb to the tidal wave of despair and temptation and angst that surrounds us on every hand, you will go back to the roots of our faith, which are stronger than any form of patriotism. I don't despise patriotism, don't misunderstand me; but there is no salvation in love of country. There is salvation only in love of Jesus Christ; and if you confuse the two, the greatest defeat will have been achieved. Remember that. Read the letters of Paul.

When you look at that fourth chapter in 2 Corinthians, the chapter with which we have been working today, you will

91

discover that this is not a faith of evasion, a faith of success, or a faith of unambiguous pleasure and delight. It is reality, a reality that believers have always been forced to face. "In the world," says the apostle John, "we shall have tribulation." Jesus says, "Be of good cheer; I have overcome the world" (John 16:33). Well, that's all very right and good for Jesus, who in fact has overcome the world, and good for him, I say again; but for us who have not yet overcome the world, John's Gospel is as true as ever it was. In the world we shall have tribulation, and anyone who promises us otherwise is either uninformed or lying, and perhaps both; and owes no allegiance to the gospel. When we face the world as believers, we face it with tribulation on every hand.

From this very pulpit my venerable predecessor Willard Sperry often used to quote his friend and colleague, Georges Tyrell, who was one of the famous Catholic modernists of the first third of the twentieth century; and in a time when World War I was still fresh and World War II was clearly on the horizon, Sperry preached week after week to congregations like this—to your grandparents, three generations removed. One of his favorite quotations of Father Tyrell's was Tyrell's definition of Christianity; and this is what Tyrell said, what Sperry quoted, and what I now quote again: "Christianity is an ultimate optimism founded upon a provisional pessimism." In this world we shall have tribulation.

So, a reasonable person—and we're all reasonable persons here, are we not? That's why we're here and not in some other church—might ask, "From where has this notion come, that Christians are entitled to a free 'get-out-of-jail' card, an exemption to the world of turmoil and tribulation?" This misreading of the Christian faith, for that is exactly what it is, comes from the fashionable, cultural faith with which we have so often confused the Christian faith. Most of us aspire to be believers in the Christian faith, but all of us to one degree or another, alas, ascribe to the cultural faith: and that cultural religion in times of prosperity is often easy and always dangerous. Be suspicious of religion in times of prosperity and ease. Why is it dangerous? It is dangerous because prosperity itself can become a terribly tempting false god and a substitute for religion; and in the name of the religion of prosperity, success, and control, most of us will do anything and almost everything, and we have.

In times of prosperity, either we make prosperity our religion, or we imagine that we can do without religion altogether. Who needs it? When turmoil happens to others, we can be mildly empathetic, perhaps even sympathetic, and maybe we can even utter that famous aphorism, "There but for the grace of God go I"; but when turmoil hits us, when we are knocked flat, when all of our securities and our cherished illusions are challenged to the breaking point, and break, then comes the great question we must both ask and answer, "What is left when everything we have is taken from us?"

What is left when everything you have is taken from you? For the last decade, on commencement morning, in my sermons to the seniors about to leave this college, I have asked questions like this: "How will you live after the fall?" I don't mean autumn; I mean the Fall. "How will you manage when trouble comes? How will you manage when you are tested and fail the test? How will you cope with frustration and fear and failure and anxiety?" Many of them have thought those to be quaint and even rude questions, perhaps the kind of rhetorical excess that preachers engage in around commencement time, a kind of raining on their parade.

Since September 11, however, these are no longer abstract, philosophical, or theoretical questions, and people have gravitated in astonishing numbers to the places where such questions are taken seriously. Every rabbi, minister, priest, imam, and spiritual leader whom I know or have heard of reports, as can I, the incredible turn toward faith in this time of our current crisis. Probably not since World War II has there been in our country such a conspicuous turn to the faith, and both our ordinary and our extraordinary services here in the last ten days bear profound witness to this. On Tuesday afternoon, September 11, the day of the terrorist attacks on the World Trade Centers and the Pentagon, and the downing of the plane in Pennsylvania, we saw thousands in the Yard in an ecumenical witness; and on Friday of that same week we saw almost as many here at a service of prayer and remembrance, on a day especially designated a national day of prayer and remembrance. Last Sunday's service was like Easter day, and this one is very close to it. The daily service of morning prayer in Appleton Chapel is nearly standing-room-only, and this past week the president of this university asked if he could come and speak at morning prayer on Friday, thus proving beyond all shadow of a doubt that there is a God. With his opening words from our lectern, he said that this was the last place he expected to find himself so early in his administration. This is from a secular man who, by the standards of this secular place, is as close to God as many aspire to reach.

These are extraordinary times; this is an extraordinary moment. We are witnessing extraordinary things, and I ask you this, Is it not an incredible irony that in the face of the most terrible and tangible facts available to us, the destruction of those monuments to material success—the brutally physical worldly reality with the violence before our very eyes—that men and women instinctively turn to the very thing that cannot be seen? They turn not to the reality of the visible but to the reality of the invisible which, when compared to what can be seen, ultimately endures. Seeking faith amidst the ruins is the subtext of these days. There's a terrible parable there, that as the very temple to which we offered our secular worship is destroyed before us we seek the God who precedes and who follows these temples made and destroyed by human hands. People are seeking inner strength beyond the outer turmoil: that is what I see and that is what I hear on every hand, in every paper, in every magazine, on every talk show, and on everybody's lips.

In light of this, the question "Where is God?" seems almost irrelevant. This was the question of the day for the religion editor of *The Boston Globe* last weekend, and a host of my clerical colleagues attempted an answer or two. I was not asked—another proof of the existence of God—but had I been, I would have said what I now say to you, which is that it was the wrong question. The question is not where God is when disaster strikes; the real and interesting question is where you were before disaster struck? Where were you two weeks ago? Three weeks ago? Where will you be three weeks from now, or four weeks from now? God has not forgotten you, but is it not reasonable to suggest that before September 11 many of us had forgotten God? God is where God always is and has always been; it is we who have to account for our absence.

Be certain of one thing, however, we should not be embarrassed that now in adversity we seek the God whom we had forgotten in prosperity, for what is God for if he is not to be there when we seek him? We should not be embarrassed that in trouble we have remembered one profound theological truth, that God is to be found where God is most needed—in trouble, sorrow, sickness, adversity, and even in death itself. Over and over and over again the psalms make this point, as we sang in the sermon hymn, in paraphrase of Psalm 46: "God is our refuge and strength: a very present help in trouble."

Isn't this Luther's point in his great hymn, "A Mighty Fortress Is Our God"?

> Let goods and kindred go,
> This mortal life also;
> The body they may kill;
> God's truth abideth still,
> His kingdom is forever.

You don't have to be a Lutheran to know the truth of that. Then remember that one of the few bright spots in the

National Cathedral Service of Prayer and Remembrance one week ago came in Billy Graham's sermon when he quoted the old hymn "How Firm a Foundation":

Fear not, I am with thee, O be not dismayed,
For I am thy God and will still give thee aid;
I'll strengthen and help thee, and cause thee to stand,
Upheld by my righteous, omnipotent hand.

Those hymns weren't written yesterday. They were not written by people who did not know turmoil. They were written by people who in the midst of outer turmoil had inner strength.

This past week, as I've thought about this morning and my obligations toward you, two images have flashed in my mind. One was the indelible image of those burning towers and those terrible encounters with the airplanes, a kind of conflict of our own magnificent technologies coming together in a horrible parody of our skills and our strengths. That was one image. The other goes back to one of my favorite movies, which will identify all of my phobias and predilections and will also give away my age. Between Dunkirk and Pearl Harbor there was produced one great film, *Mrs. Miniver.* Those of you who know it know that I'm referring to that last scene in the bombed-out church on a Sunday morning, where, with the window destroyed and the cross standing in the broken window, and the people of the congregation ripped apart by Hitler's bombing of their little village, yet still they sing, "Children of the heavenly king/As we journey sweetly sing." I know it was a great propaganda film, I know it was designed to rouse the souls and the spirits of the British people; I know it was the British version of Hollywood, with Walter Pidgeon and Greer Garson. I know all of that, and I believe it! So did the British people, and so do you need to believe that in that construction somewhere rests the image of the God who was with us at the most terrible moment of our time. The answer to the question "Where is God?" is that God is where God is always—by the side of those who need him. He is not in front to lead, not behind to push, not above to protect, but beside us to get us through: "Beside us to guide us/Our God with us joining." I cannot imagine those heroic firefighters and policemen and workers and volunteers, amidst the rubble of Ground Zero in New York, indulging in the luxurious theological speculation about where God might or might not be. They *know* where God is: he is right there with them, enabling them, empowering them, and strengthening them, even when hope itself has died. If you want to know where God is, do not ask the prosperous. Ask the suffering. Ask the sorrowing. Ask those who are acquainted with grief.

In the *Book of Common Prayer* there is a collect which begins, "God of all comfort. . . ." To some who don't know any better, that sounds like mere consolation; something soothing; adequate words in troubled times of turmoil and tribulation; a kind of bandage on cancer, if you will, like the "comfortable words" in the old *Book of Common Prayer,* which were not very comforting to a church and a culture that had grown too comfortable. Do you know the proper meaning of the word *comfort,* by the way? You're about to. It means to "fortify," to "strengthen," to "give courage," even "power," and not merely consolation. The God of all comfort is the One who supplies what we most lack when we most need it. As Paul puts it, he gives us sufficient capacity that when we are knocked down we are not knocked out. The God of all comfort is not the god who fights like Superman, or Rambo, or Clint Eastwood, or any of our conventional cultural heroes. The God of all comfort is the One who gives inner power and strength to those who would be easily outnumbered, outmaneuvered, outpowered by the conventional forces and the conventional wisdom. Inner strength is what is required when in the midst of turmoil; we do not know what to do with our outward power and our outward might.

Let us also not forget one powerful fact that we are tempted to forget, which is that the world has always been a dangerous and precarious place. That we have just discovered this terrible fact for ourselves does not make it any less true or any less dangerous. Outer turmoil is no longer the fate that falls to others: the shrinking world that has allowed us to export technology abroad has now, alas, permitted terror to be imported to us. The great question is how we stand and how we manage in a world now less brave, now less new than ever it was.

Inner strength, I believe, comes from the sure conviction that God has placed us in the world to do the work of life, and not of death. This is what Saint Paul says in Corinthians. "We are always facing death," he writes, "but this means that [we] know more and more of life" (2 Corinthians 4:11 JBP). Faith is not the opposite either of doubt or of death, but the means whereby we face and endure doubt and death, and overcome our fear of them. Our inner faith as believers comes from the sure conviction that neither death nor doubt nor fear is the last word. This is not a policy statement for the nation; this is a sure conviction for Christian believers. Therefore, because we believe that, and because that belief is testified to by the experience of our ancestors in the faith and our contemporaries who labor beside us and for God in the rubble, we are able to endure. We are able to go through the worst for the best, come what may. Endurance is what it takes when you have nothing left. Phillips Brooks once said that we do not pray for lighter loads, but for greater strength to bear the loads we are given. Heavy loads have been placed upon us in these days, and even greater burdens and sacrifices are to come. Of that there can be no doubt; and, like Jesus in the garden, we would be less than human if we did not pray that this cup might pass us by—but it won't. The real issue for us, then, as it was for Jesus, is, how do we manage?

Inner strength in the midst of turmoil, I suggest, is not simply stoic endurance and perseverance, important as they are, especially in tough, demanding times. Nor is inner strength simply a form of mind over matter, a kind of moral escapism that says that you "may have captured my body, but my mind is free." It's not only either of those. When I tried to think of what it was, I remembered a story told by Dr. Ernest Gordon, who for many years was dean of the chapel at Princeton, and more famous because of his book about his captivity on the River Kwai during World War II. In that Japanese prison camp, Ernest Gordon said that he and his fellow British who were captives were initially very religious, reading their Bibles, praying, singing hymns, witnessing and testifying to their faith, and hoping and expecting that God would reward them and fortify them for their faith by freeing them or at least mitigating their captivity. God didn't deliver, however, and the men became both disillusioned and angry, and some even faithless. They gave up on the outward display of their faith; but after a while, Gordon says, the men, responding to the needs of their fellows—caring for them, protecting the weaker ones, and in some cases dying for one another—began to discern something of a spirit of God in their midst. It was not a revival of religion in the conventional sense, but rather the discovery that religion was not what you believed but what you did for others when it seemed that you could do nothing at all. It was compassion that gave them their inner strength, and it was from their inner strength that their compassion came. I owe this insight to Dr. Leonard Griffith, from *Illusions of Our Culture.*

Could it be that amidst the cries of vengeance and violence and warfare, and the turmoil that is attempting to sweep us all up in the calamity of these days, the inner strength we so desperately seek is the strength that comes from compassion, from hearing and heeding the cry of the other?

In one of Theodore Parker Ferris's books, I found underlined these words about strength: "Some people's strength is all drawn from themselves. They are like isolated pools with limited reserves. Others are more like rivers. They do not produce or contain the power, but it flows through them, like blood through the body. The more they give, the more they are able to draw in. That strength is theirs, but it is not their own."

Then the author says, in words that I wish were mine: "The strength that God gives is available to those who care for others, for they are showing the spirit of Jesus. The power of God's spirit fortifies them" (Hugh Martin; *The Beatitudes;* Harper & Brothers; 1953).

Can it be that inner strength is not simply the capacity to endure, but to give? Can it be that compassion is superior to power? Can it be that amid the turmoil of that violent crowd on Good Friday, from his inner strength Jesus showed compassion? He forgave his enemies, he reunited his friends, and he redeemed the criminal.

When in the midst of turmoil and calamity you seek the inner strength that helps you not only to endure but to overcome, do not look for what you can get; look, rather, for what you have been given and for what you can give. We begin with calamity, but we end with compassion. Remember the quotation that Theodore Ferris had underlined: "The strength that God gives is available for those who care for others."

Thirteen

A Sermon for the Fifteenth Sunday After Pentecost

James Howell
First United Methodist Church
Davidson, North Carolina

(Psalm 102)

In a normal week, I would be in touch with one or two other preachers. Basically, in the course of a week we email or call each other from around the country or wherever and say, "What are you going to tell them on Sunday?" This week I did not have just one or two conversations; I had, I don't know, maybe fifty, and even about what passage, out of all of God's Word, would we alight upon to talk about today. It is a different kind of Sunday—a different kind of sermon. Usually for me, when there is something of great public import, my style would be to try to preach a fairly fiery sermon and say, "Let's charge out and go get them!" Of course, since Tuesday, we've heard plenty of voices say, "Let's charge out and go get them!" Within hours of the tragedy, I saw Billy Graham on the Internet, and he referred to Psalm 46. He reiterated this at the National Cathedral on Friday, and we sang this today at the beginning: "A mighty fortress is our God. A bulwark never failing." The mountains may totter, the nations may rage, but God is a very present help in times of trouble.

It's a good text.

I was down at Channel 3 the other day with a pastor. We had a Bible open, looking for passages, and the pastor said, "I'm thinking about this obscure story in Luke 13 where the Tower of Siloam outside Jerusalem had fallen on eighteen people and killed them. People came to Jesus and asked, 'Why did this happen?' And Jesus doesn't really answer that. Instead, he just looked at these people and said, 'Repent.' Maybe this can become an occasion for our repentance as people. People are praying in droves; they are coming to church in droves. I'm choosing not to be cynical about this. I believe we'll continue—I pray that we will continue. We need God all the time, not just when there's a tragedy."

Of course some preachers have tried to finesse this thing and say that it was God's will somehow—God's punishment on somebody or another. It seems to me, if this is God's punishment on anybody, the only one it makes sense to me might be the bankers, because the Bible is clear: "You shall not lend money at interest." This grinds the poor into deeper poverty. The Bible says this repeatedly. So you could say this was the reason. Or, was it Jerry Falwell, who said that it was the feminists' fault? This is stupid! It's not God's will at all. If it's God's will, one thing we're relieved of is trying to find Osama bin Laden, unless we want to find him so that we can throw a ticker tape parade for him and say, "Thank you so much for doing God's will." This is contrary in the worse possible way to God's will. Everyone recognizes that.

The text that I've chosen to talk on is a little bit obscure, a little bit oddball: Psalm 102. It's a little more familiar to Roman Catholics. I think it's one of what they call their Seven Penitential Psalms, psalms that the ancient Israelites used during times of intense grief—during times of intense fear and sorrow—when the depth of their grief was almost beyond words. They would use this prayer. Let me read the beginning of it to you:

> Let my cry come to you[, O Lord;].
> Do not hide your face . . .
> My days pass away like smoke,
>   and my bones burn like a furnace.
> My heart is stricken and withered . . .
> I [forget] to eat my bread.
> I am like an owl [among the ruins].
> I lie awake; . . .
> My enemies taunt me; . . .
> I eat ashes like bread.

That line, "I am like an owl [among the ruins]," has always intrigued me. I don't really know much about owls, but they do not seem to be the happiest of birds. They do not sing sweet songs, as do some other birds. They do not have a beautiful feather, as do some other birds. They are strange; they are awake when everyone else is asleep. They have a different kind of vision—their eyes are wide open in the dark, and they seem to be able to see in the dark. Perhaps, because of this, they are associated with wisdom.

Being awake in the dark—I don't know about you, but I've been awake in the dark a lot since Tuesday, unable to sleep. It was on Wednesday night this week that I just could not get to sleep, and I was kind of wandering the house. I did something that I frequently do: I went into my son's room. I know this is stupid, but I like to go in my son's room and just watch him sleep. It's a beautiful thing; it's tender, it's calm, it's bright. Somehow I think the meaning of the universe is somehow captured in a sleeping child.

But on Wednesday night all was not calm, all was not bright. I watched my son sleeping, and I had this bizarre urge to throw my body on top of him to shelter him somehow from the falling debris of a world crumbling around us. As I thought about doing that, I began to think that on Tuesday there were people we will never know about who threw their body on top of someone and made some valiant effort to save the life of probably a stranger. We will never know their story. God knows, but we will not know; but we may be sure that that happened. We see now the noble people we were made to be by God. People who can make great sacrifices. People who can reach out to strangers. As I kept watching my son sleep, I was thunderstruck when I realized that somewhere in northern Virginia, in southern Maryland, in northern New Jersey and Manhattan, in western Connecticut, that there is some little boy, or some little girl, who no longer has a father or a mother to come into the room and watch him or her sleep. I wonder if those children are sleeping at all? Or, are they tossing and turning, soaking their bed with their tears. I do not know their names, but I know their hearts; we can fathom their pain. We just can't say, "Thank goodness it wasn't me." There is a child sleeping with no father or mother.

I wanted to wake up my son. He'd seen all of the news, and I wanted to wake him up and say, "Oh, my precious little boy, do not worry. The world is really safe after all. Nothing like this could ever happen again. You're safe; you're secure; don't worry." But of course that would be to lie to my son.

I heard Donald Rumsfeld at a press conference. Some reporter was asking, "Can you guarantee this will never happen again?" And Rumsfeld, with no bravado at all, said, "No, we cannot guarantee this. We are vulnerable."

We were vulnerable before Tuesday. I must be the only person on this planet who was not surprised by what happened. I was shocked; I was appalled; amazed; all of those things. But I was not surprised. I have expected this kind of thing and worse for many years. We have been vulnerable. We are vulnerable people. We couldn't pretend any longer as of Tuesday. As George Santayana put it in one of his poems when one of his friends had died: "And I am grown much older in a day." I think we grew older on Tuesday. This vulnerability cuts two ways. There's the negative side of it: you worry how this is going to affect us? I think I watched that TV videotape of a plane slamming into a building too many times—it's now rerunning itself in my head—that's why I have trouble sleeping. What is that doing to children?

One of our children was at the elementary school the next day when some jerk phoned in some kind of threat, and the children spent three hours outside the building. When one little girl came home, she said, "Mom, we were outside for three hours." Her mom asked, "Why?" And she said, "An airplane nearly crashed into our school." How do we rid our self of this kind of torment and yet not lose the good side of realizing our vulnerability? Once we discover that we are vulnerable, things that mattered before don't matter as much. We're able to make sacrifices for each other; we're able to reach out; we're able to love. When this news came, you couldn't just sit alone in your office, you had to watch this with somebody else, you had to get on the phone, you had to get together with those whom you love.

People said, "James, you ought to leave your kids at school. That's the best place for them." I wanted them home. I wanted them with me. I had to call my friends and family. What did people say in those pained last calls out of the World Trade Center? They said, "I just want you to know that I love you very, very, very much." You see, our vulnerability makes us tender, it helps us to love to realize our need for God.

Fourteen

All Creation Groans

Stephen Johnson
Abilene Christian University

(Romans 8:18-25)

> We know that the whole creation has been groaning . . . right up to the present time. (Romans 8:22 NIV)

Not long ago, my grandfather, who had not been feeling well, received test results that told us he had pancreatic cancer. No treatment would help. His days were numbered. A few weeks later, I pulled away from a busy schedule and traveled to see my grandfather. He was declining rapidly. During one of his more lucid moments one morning, I knelt at his bedside and held his hand. He looked into my face and forced a slight grin. "Stephen," he said, then he spoke words to me that could only be construed as the kind of blessing a grandfather gives to his oldest grandchild. I then watched him close his eyes and begin to struggle again through the pain of his illness. And something deep within me groaned.

A good friend and brother called late one night. When I answered the phone; he began to sob. He attempted to speak, but sometimes the words just wouldn't come out. I waited through the sobbing, my stomach twisting into a knot that then rose to become a lump in my throat. At last, he began to explain the pain of his predicament. And something deep within me groaned.

You have been there perhaps—or you will be. That moment when it strikes you, as it did the tow truck driver in the movie *Grand Canyon*, who pulls up as a group of street thugs have surrounded a man and are about to beat him severely and strip his car. The driver, in an attempt at diplomacy, takes the leader of the gang aside and says, "Man, the world ain't supposed to work like this. Maybe you don't know that, but this ain't the way it's supposed to be. I'm supposed to be able to do my job without askin' you if I can. And that dude is supposed to be able to wait with his car without you rippin' him off. Everything's supposed to be different than what it is here." It's that moment when it strikes you—"the world ain't supposed to work like this . . . this ain't the way it's supposed to be" and deep within something groans.

It happens over and over again—to an individual here, a family there; sometimes a small community holds an experience in common. And suddenly, where the world once seemed all put together and life all right side up, things seem topsy-turvy, shattered into about a million pieces. There is no mistaking one's brokenness within the brokenness of this world. And in about a hundred different ways we say, "The world ain't supposed to work like this."

This, it seems to me, is what is remarkable about the events of September 11. Not just that it happened, a remarkable enough thing in itself, but that it happened to us all. Because once in a while, not so often, there comes a moment like this when an entire nation gasps in horror, is sent reeling so that the collective experience of an entire nation is a deep groaning. "Man, the world ain't supposed to work like this," we say. Something is not right. The illusion is unveiled for what it is, and it becomes painfully clear that we are not the arbiters of our own salvation, our own security, our well-being regardless of the amount of military power we possess, the economic resources at our disposal, or the brilliant technology we have mastered. It becomes painfully clear just how vulnerable we all are in this world.

We know that the whole creation [groans] . . . [even] we . . . , who have the firstfruits of the Spirit groan inwardly. (Romans 8:22, 23)

So here we stand—we who are called out to be the people of God. Here we stand in a moment that brings into sharp focus the essence of that calling. It is we who are called to stand in the midst of the rubble of our invincibility, the ruins of our self-confidence, or the chaos of our deflated hopes— a tragedy that stretches far beyond New York City and Washington, D.C., a tragedy that has happened and will continue to happen countless times and in countless ways. It is we who are called to stand and name the thing rightly: "Here, you see, the whole creation groans—broken, fallen, frail."

And the good news, the gospel that is spoken here is not "It will be all right." Because in a most fundamental way, it is not all right and will not be all right. The good news, the gospel that is spoken here is not even the reassurance that "We're on top of this. We'll track down those responsible and set the record straight." No. The good news, the gospel that is spoken here is not that, with a little extra effort on all our parts, we can make the world a better, safer place. Because we cannot. Our calling is not to smooth over, explain away, psychology soothe, or give easy trite answers so that we can all cope. Our calling is to stand in solidarity with the world in its brokenness and name the thing rightly, "See, all creation groans."

And from that place to give words to the prayer that is intuitively within us all—a deep longing for nothing less than a new heaven and a new earth where there will be no more mourning or crying or pain, for the old order of things has not been fixed up, made better, a little more livable, but the old order of things has passed away. We stand in this moment to pray, "Even so, come quickly, Lord Jesus," as all creation groans.

This is the word of the Lord. Thanks be to God!

Fifteen

Whose Agenda Matters?

Mark Labberton
First Presbyterian Church of Berkeley

(Matthew 10; John 6)

In light of September 11, the relevance and urgency of this brief series of sermons on the first question of the Heidelberg Catechism amazes me. Although written in the sixteenth century, and therefore separated in so many important ways from this moment, it affirms a bedrock Christian faith, perhaps especially needed in a time such as this.

Q: What is your only comfort, in life and in death?

A: That I belong—body and soul, in life and in death—not to myself but to my faithful Savior, Jesus Christ, who at the cost of his own blood has fully paid for all my sins and has completely freed me from the dominion of the devil; that he protects me so well that without the will of my Father in heaven not a hair can fall from my head; indeed, that everything must fit his purpose for my salvation. Therefore, by his Holy Spirit, he also assures me of eternal life, and makes me wholeheartedly willing and ready from now on to live for him.

Painfully, even dramatically, we are concentrating today on the phrase *"that he protects me so well that without the will of my Father in heaven not a hair can fall from my head; indeed, that everything must fit his purpose for my salvation."*

Just in case there was any desire here today to consider (again!) the problem of evil, this phrase helps to frame the issue. Of course with a full twenty minutes to solve the problem of pain, we might be wishing we could tackle something a little bigger!

The challenge of suffering and God's will is a challenge which this last set of days has brought into focus. The problem of pain is and has been reproduced over and over and over again throughout the course of human history. Pre-Christian philosophers have struggled with the issue and certainly that is so in the days since Christ. What we're given in Scripture is no easy answer, no plain schematic drawing in which the relationship between suffering and God's will are outlined. No such explanation exists in the Bible. Instead, what we find in Scripture is the full agony of the questions human experience raises. And alongside that, God's unexpected and peculiar response.

As we ourselves suffer this week and feel the problem of evil on our own turf, we need to hold on to the fact that the problem of evil is much bigger and more complex of course than even this. As a matter of scale, in this one site in New York in the destruction of the World Trade Centers, its scope was stunningly described this week in *The Chronicle* as a physical loss equal to—if not greater than—the amount of office space in all of San Francisco. That is the scale of physical destruction, let alone human destruction, that overwhelms our imaginations. Reports are now that approximately 6,300 to 6,500 people are missing, an extraordinary degree of suffering and human loss.

Imagine, however, that the potential for other terrorist strikes had been fulfilled. Let's consider how it would seem if instead of 6,500, that losses had been between 10,000 to

20,000 on September 11. And then let's imagine that that had occurred again on September 12. And again on September 13. And September 14. And September 15. September 16. And every day, day by day, 10,000 to 20,000 people were killed, all the way until November 11. For eight to ten weeks, 10,000 to 20,000 per day. A total of 800,000 or more people. We would call that Rwanda, 1994. In horror and outrage, 6,500 people are killed in America in a series of extraordinary events, and the world is riveted and grief-struck. In Rwanda, 10,000 to 20,000 people a day for eight weeks are slaughtered, and if the world even acknowledged that fact, it was often masked and understated. It was relatively easy for us to cope with; it was just absorbed in our lives. Of course it was not visibly witnessed by us in the same way. It is not cast across the world in every CNN broadcast twenty-four hours a day, day in and day out. And, far more tellingly, it was not on our soil.

As we affirm today that God "protects [us] so well that without the will of [our] Father in heaven not a hair can fall from [our] heads," we are remembering that thousands upon thousands of those killed in Rwanda, and many of those no doubt killed in New York, Pennsylvania, and Washington, D.C., were not only human brothers and sisters, but most especially part of our family in Christ. So when we face the problem of evil, we need to remember those in the Trade Centers, but also those in Rwanda. We remember those innocent lost whose deaths break our hearts, but we must include ourselves inside the problem of evil as those whose hearts don't necessarily break for strangers, even when they are our brother or sister.

If we are going to hear our catechism and hear our Scripture as the good news we need them to be, let's not for a moment step away from the problem of evil. Let's believe that if, in fact, the gospel of Jesus Christ is sufficient for the world, it means looking squarely at issues like Rwanda, its suffering, and its death. But Third World suffering does not get the world's attention like our own. That's part of the problem of evil too. A horror as staggering in its scope as Rwanda gets ignored, ignored by those of us who are often sadly busy protecting our lives from looking at such pain. We are busy stepping away from the world scene, and the political scene, military scene, or social scene.

We dwell in individualist America as individualistic Christians and think principally about the reality of suffering as it's born inside people's lives, the reality of suffering and pain that unfolds because of psychological suffering, suffering that decimates a life from inside, and that can decimate a series of other lives, damaging whole family systems from one generation to the next. Or we remember those innocents whose physical conditions from disease, illness, or injury leave them profoundly in need, so broken that their suffering is easily their occupation, an innocent suffering borne every day of their lives.

To all this, Scripture gives no easy explanation. But what the Scripture does offer, and what the catechism upholds, are affirmations that at the very least orient us to the landscape of suffering while offering us genuine hope. Scripture affirms two things that seem so difficult to hold together: we live in a world of suffering *and* we trust the God whose suffering love protects us in our suffering. So what about the hairs on our head?

How do these two affirmations actually exist side by side? Perhaps one of the places we should turn is the context in which the image or metaphor about the hairs on our head arises. This reference appears in Jesus' teaching in the Gospel of Matthew, as well as in Luke. In Matthew 10, the context holds these two themes of suffering and protection clearly together. Jesus is instructing his disciples, following the Sermon on the Mount, on a variety of issues. He is talking to them about the reality, the assurance, that as disciples of his they will suffer. He goes on at some length about suffering and persecution and pain that will be a consequence

113

of belonging to him. Starting with verse 26 of Matthew 10, Jesus says:

> So have no fear of them; for nothing is covered up that will not be uncovered, and nothing secret that will not become known. What I say to you in the dark, tell in the light; and what you hear whispered, proclaim from the housetops. Do not fear those who kill the body but cannot kill the soul; rather fear him who can destroy both soul and body in hell. Are not two sparrows sold for a penny? Yet not one of them will fall to the ground apart from your Father. And even the hairs of your head are all counted. So do not be afraid; you are of more value than many sparrows. (Matthew 10:26-31)

What does it mean to affirm the words of the catechism, then, that the protection of the Father is with us, so that even a hair from our head would not fall but that it be by the will of the Father, and eventually work out for the salvation of my soul? You see, if the Christian faith has meaning, it's got to be able to step into this question.

It was Chuck Colson who said that American Christianity is often three thousand miles wide and an inch deep! The reality of suffering leaves every mind undone. But a faith that is three thousand miles wide and an inch deep will surely not be sufficient for facing the reality of suffering. What events like those of the last several days have done in part is something extremely important. These events peel back any illusion of some kind of naïve protection, any illusion that somehow what life is really about is skating through and being able to find a way in middle-class American life, to no longer feel as though suffering is really our experience. We have the opportunity—perhaps just for a moment, and perhaps we will anesthetize ourselves against it—but we have the opportunity to dare to look at, to allow ourselves to feel, to truly experience in a way that perhaps none of us has experienced before, the depth of what that kind of exposure and vulnerability to suffering really means.

It may or may not have actually been someone we know who was directly affected by the events in New York or Washington D.C., but we are nevertheless affected. We are, perhaps just for the moment, able to identify with so much of the world that suffers every day; for example, the one billion or more in absolute poverty. We have the opportunity to identify just for a moment, in our own particular way with overwhelming circumstances that are beyond us, a suffering that impinges on us not, by our own choice that we don't deserve, didn't seek, can't resolve. We have a chance, a chance to begin asking ourselves, What does it mean to live and confess our Christian faith as we live in a world where life and its suffering is not chosen, and not able to be removed by buying our way out, counseling our way out, politicizing our way out? And we need to ask ourselves now, What does faith, and in particular our faith in Christ, do for us and for our world in the face of suffering that is of this kind? of this scale? and in no way new or greater because of the acts of September 11, but evil that can be seen and experienced by millions and millions of people every day and throughout the generations?

The God of the Bible is a God who knows, shares, and suffers with the world. There is a caricature alive in society and even in the church, with at best a two-dimensional, maybe even only one-dimensional vision of God that many try to preserve. But evil helpfully exposes and destroys such an idol. This anemic, shallow gloss seeks somehow to remove God from this messy world. But what one has, then, is a God who has little real relationship to the God of the Bible. For the God made known in Scripture is the suffering-with-us-and-for-us God. Reading the Bible closely, one encounters a God who pursues us in our brokenness, a God who chases Israel generation by generation precisely in order to stand with people in real need, and who provides for people who wander and wonder if they have lost God's attention. God does not stand far removed, but comes to bear with us. That

115

sense is intensified as we walk through the Bible. We see a God whose heart is broken, a God whose heart aches for the suffering of the world.

We also hear of a God in power who has also chosen to create a world of freedom, a world in which human beings can choose evil or choose good, in which many forms—not all forms, but many forms—of suffering are chosen as a consequence of our poor exercise of our humanity. Having been made in the image of God with the capacity for goodness means that we also bear the capacity for at least equal evil. If we choose evil over goodness, God in his power and mercy allows us that freedom, but he is never inattentive to that. He comes as the shepherd. This affirmation is of a God who, as shepherd, comes to bear the suffering of those that are in need.

This is the God who ultimately in Jesus Christ comes to stand at the vortex of evil, to bear in his own life and death the consequences of what evil and suffering are about. If we think of God, as Scripture instructs us, we now think of God suffering, of the suffering God, of a God who stands in and amidst and with and for a world that suffers. And it was Jesus' understanding that he had come to suffer, not only that he was called to suffer but also is calling a people to follow him who, like him, will suffer. He goes to the cross and allows literally the hairs of his head to fall in suffering by God's will and on our behalf. In doing so, Jesus also calls those who belong to him to be willing to suffer both for the sake of identifying with those in need and for the sake of doing and entering into the work of love, which is the suffering work to which the church of Jesus Christ has been called.

A church three thousand miles wide and an inch deep can't and won't live this way. The church of America does not like this calling, and often the church around the world and throughout history has not liked it, either. The American church in particular has often done everything possible to try to anesthetize itself against suffering, to try to find ways of packaging the Christian life so that suffering is not a part of discipleship. We presume as a first principle that surely God wouldn't want us to suffer; that's what makes the church in America the church in America!

Surely what God is about and is trying to do is to help us be happy. And if we care about the world beyond, some versions of the American gospel can sound like we emit the message to suffering people, "God wants you to be happy, too, just like we are!"

There is no evidence in the Bible that God wants us to be happy. That's just not there! Joy? Now that's something God wants us to know. Hope? That's something God cares about deeply. Happiness? Happiness in the sense of carefree delight, no problems, easy, no sense of conscience, no particular sense of worry or burden—that's not in the Bible.

To identify with the God of the Bible is to identify with someone who identifies with those who suffer. We have the opportunity in these days to realize that if our faith hasn't stepped into those sorts of issues, hasn't stepped into an identification with an agenda of a God who bears the weight of the world, and invites us into what Paul calls "the fellowship of Christ's sufferings"; if our faith can't take us there, then I would dare to say that it is not biblical faith, or that if it is biblical faith, it is radically immature faith. The faith that is mature, the faith that God of the Scripture calls us to grow into, is a faith in which we understand and at least stand with the God who stands with those who suffer. And therefore we can anticipate and expect to take up our cross and to follow Jesus Christ.

It is in that context that Jesus, in the Gospel reading from John this morning, says, "I have come to do the will of my Father." And what is the will of God for Jesus? To suffer, and to die, and to rise again, that the world might know real hope. And what is the will of God for us? That we might enter into Christ's sufferings and understand them on our behalf, but also that we carry out the work of the kingdom, which is going to involve for us in part entering into the suffering of the world. Scripture daringly points to the God who sends us into suffering and not away from it.

So how does protection and suffering come together in biblical faith and in the catechism? Well, it comes together in part by acknowledging that God embodies both affirmations—embodies the experience of suffering on the cross and embodies in the cross itself the suffering that becomes the means of our protection. In the mystery of God's own love, those two things come together simultaneously in the cross, which is both God's suffering and God's protection. They are the same event in the experience of Jesus Christ. So, different from but parallel to Jesus, disciples can anticipate that to follow God in a world like ours is going to engage us in that very place where the cross becomes the definition of living a human life in a context where we both suffer and find protection, where we identify with suffering and offer protection.

It is interesting that our morning phrase from the Heidelberg Catechism says that God protects me so well that without the will of my Father in heaven not a hair can fall from my head. This was written in the sixteenth century, and by the seventeenth century that language becomes distilled in what I would call a kind of high Calvinism. What I mean is the emergence of a kind of vision of God as the divine manager of earthly hairs in which every single issue of the hairs on my head gets micromanaged by the God of heaven. Is that our sense of what this catechism affirms? When Jesus uses this image in Matthew 10, he doesn't use it in this micromanaged sense. I think what Jesus is affirming is that there is no detail of your life or mine in which God is disengaged, unaffected, dispassionate, or unrelated. I do not hear Jesus teaching that God manages the movement of every hair, but that God who sees and cares is affected by all the realities of our lives, including in that sense, metaphorically, every hair on our head.

118

There is a radical difference between suggesting that God micromanages every hair, and the sense that, instead, what God does is enter into every element of our experience. To me, it is Jesus' affirmation that God does the latter—that God who is never dispassionate, never disconnected, never separated even from the falling of every hair on our heads. It's that God whom Jesus says will work through every experience "for my salvation," God's grand agenda.

Now *salvation* in the Bible is a very rich and enormous word. But again, often in our own particular theological framework it can so easily become reduced to something no bigger than "Jesus and me." It's just about inward pietism; it's just about am I saved or am I not saved? Have I signed the commitment card, gone down the sawdust trail? Have I raised my hand at the meeting? Am I saved? And while all that is very important, very important indeed, it can be often very puny.

Salvation, in the language of Scripture, is a word that ultimately embodies the process of your and my and our world being remade in the image of Jesus Christ. This is the grander work of salvation, which is to be a part in the fashioning of a whole new creation, a new heaven and a new earth. What our reading from John and our affirmation through the catechism affirms is that God can use any and every experience of my life, and of yours, and of the world's to accomplish this grand work of salvation.

God can use even the greatest evil, which I would argue is ultimately the evil of Christ's death, to bring about the salvation of the world. It is a work which engages me, it includes me, but it is staggeringly bigger than I am. It's not a protection that causes me to just run away and say, "Well, I am protected under the umbrella of God's love," or "I don't need to worry about what's happening in the world or where things are happening or what suffering is going on, because I at least am in the Kingdom and therefore I am safe." While that may be true if we are in Christ, such self-serving hiding is not mature.

119

What we are called to is a maturity of faith in which we realize that our salvation is not only for our sake but also for the sake—as Jesus says in Matthew, and again here in John—of enacting what it means to live a safe life; and what does that mean? Protecting me and my own? Or understanding, as the catechism asserts so wonderfully, that "I belong—body and soul, in life and in death—not to myself, but to my faithful Savior, Jesus Christ."

And what has my faithful Savior, Jesus Christ, called me to do? To take up my cross and to follow Him. So when we think about the suffering that we are going through, we think about the vulnerability that we feel, we have a chance to identify in a deeper and different level what it really means to be a person in need of protection. But in that very moment we have the chance not only to affirm our faith but to stand with and for a God who carries that burden, who screams out against that injustice, and who also calls us as the people of God to live in a way that demonstrates that we know a God who suffers and who protects. Our God protects us in suffering.

In such an affirmation there is mystery indeed. There are so many elements of the problem of evil that this understanding does not clearly resolve, elements of an answer to the problem of evil that I don't begin to think that this sermon adequately addresses. What can be held on to is knowing and trusting in the God who holds these mysteries and who has in Christ given us sufficient clarity about God's identification with suffering, and God's means of protection—to begin to say, like Job, "I know my redeemer liveth," and because I know my Redeemer suffers for the sake of a suffering world. That Redeemer can and must be followed into places of suffering and pain in my life and also into the world.

Has this been a wake-up call for the American church to mature, to wake from its self-serving illusions of happiness? Has this been a wake-up call for the American church to begin to understand the depth of our own need to grow up in Christ? Will we look at the reality of our own gifts that God has provided and acknowledge that they have been given for the sake of being given away? To be offered for the sake of doing the work of identifying with those in suffering and in need around the world? Or, will we just say, "Phew, we've survived, we're alive, we're okay"?

If we just do that, another opportunity to identify with the One whom we call our Savior and Lord will have been missed. And millions upon millions upon millions of people around the world will have no greater glimpse through us, or perhaps through the church in other places in the world, of a God who does understand the reality of suffering, who does provide protection, and whose ultimate protection will work out for the salvation of the world. For how are they to be assured of the suffering protection of God if those who are among its recipients here hoard it and fail to extend it in mercy to a world in pain?

May we who follow Jesus Christ find comfort as we grow up in this time of lost innocence, this time of pain and anguish. May we allow ourselves to become the disciples that Jesus invites us to be, where salvation is being worked out in us, but also being worked out through us for the sake of the world.

Sixteen

A Christian Response to September 11, 2001

Todd Lake
Baylor University

(Isaiah 53:5-7)

On the morning of September 11—a date we will never forget—our campus community suddenly found itself gravitating to the large screen TVs in the student center and to other sets hastily turned on in offices across campus. All of us who had been going about our individual lives began coming together, piling up here and there like driftwood on the shore during a gathering storm. We watched the tragedy unfold in New York and Washington and Pennsylvania, and we watched each other to see how we were reacting. Shortly after the second World Trade Center tower collapsed, someone in the group of students I was with said, "We need to pray," and so we did. And in the hours and days that followed, we organized prayer meetings across campus. Thousands of students, faculty, and staff came together to pray for those who were suffering and dying, those who were waiting for news of a loved one, and those who had just gotten tragic news that was too much to bear. We prayed for the rescue workers working night and day, and for the families of the firefighters and police who had run toward the pain and suffering even as others were fleeing it.

But following the first wave of prayers came a rising tide of anger and revenge. How could anyone do this! They must pay for this! I spoke with one good Christian student the day after the attacks who said that we "should bomb Afghanistan and turn it into a parking lot." In a survey conducted Saturday, *The New York Times* reported that 58 percent of Americans think we should go after the terrorists even if "thousands and thousands of innocent people are killed in the process." Though this was not a survey of just Christians, I suspect that the results would not be dramatically different if we were to poll only church members. Think of all the husbands and wives whose hearts have been ripped away from them in the loss of their spouses. Think of how carefully these enormously evil acts were planned and plotted. These were not crimes of passion, but cold-blooded murder on a scale that dwarfs even Pearl Harbor.

Bloodshed on this grand scale demands that someone pay. And we Christians know that better than anyone: "Jesus paid it all, all to him I owe." It's at times like these we find out if we really believe what we sing in our hymnals and read in our Bibles. Scripture says that the Lord laid on him the iniquity of us all. It is easy to imagine God forgiving our petty gossiping and small-scale greediness. But can we imagine that the death of one person, on one cross, atoned for sins as monstrous as these? Yet if all that needed forgiving were venial sins, the Son of God would not have needed to become human and die on a cross, screaming out, "My God, my God, why have you forsaken me?" At that moment the unbearable weight of all human sin from the creation of the world to the end of time became Christ's agonizing burden.

Martin Luther, the great Reformer of the sixteenth century, would ask his students, "Who is the most sinful person who ever lived?" Some would say, "Pilate," and others "Judas." Luther answered, "Jesus Christ, because 'he who knew no sin became sin for us.' " Jesus is the scapegoat for all of the evil in the world, so we need not look to exact vengeance a second time.

Does God, then, demand immediate forgiveness by those still reeling from the worst attack ever on our fellow citizens? Is it not cruel, too callous, to call for forgiveness while the hunt for survivors continues in the wake of this unparalleled brutality? If forgiving others were a burden on those called to forgive, then it would indeed be heartless to demand it now. But forgiveness is not a burden for the grieving, but the first step on the path to healing. As Christian author Anne Lamott says, not forgiving others and expecting them to suffer is like drinking rat poison and waiting for the rat to die. Jesus, in the sight of his tormentors and in the midst of his agony, cried out from the cross, "Father, forgive them, they know not what they do."

We can only claim to be followers of Jesus if we, like our Lord, are willing to forgive. At times like these, our willingness to forgive is a unique witness to the world of the kind of God we serve. Christ knew the way of the world: "You have heard that it was said, 'You shall love your neighbor and hate your enemy,' " but, he adds, "I say to you, 'Love your enemies and pray for those who persecute you, so that you may be children of your Father in heaven' " (Matthew 5:43-45a). He also said: "For if you forgive others their trespasses, your heavenly Father will also forgive you; but if you do not forgive others, neither will your Father forgive your trespasses" (Matthew 6:14-15).

The terrorists, like us, are sinners. And they, like us, are saved by God's grace or not at all. To the terrorist on the cross next to him, Jesus said, "Today, you will be with me in paradise." Christ does not condone terrorism; in fact, he'd rather die than overlook how evil it is.

In times like these, we don't need a God who tells us from the safe distance of heaven "I love you." That is simply too hard to believe in a world like ours. If someone tries to tell me God is love, my attitude is "Prove it!" And we have a God who did just that. Instead of staying in the safety of heaven, the second Person of the Trinity took on human flesh in the womb of the virgin Mary. He was born among the poor and died among criminals. He was truly "a man of sorrows and acquainted with grief." He suffered in his body on the cross. We can comfort those in sorrow now by letting them know that God suffers with them. And though they mourn, they need not mourn like those without hope, for, when he rose from the grave, Christ triumphed over sin, death, and the devil. And yet his victory over death does not distance him from sorrow. He still bears the marks of his passion in his hands, his feet, his side. He did not go to the cross so we could avoid ours. Instead, he chose the way of the cross so we could follow him. His invitation is not, "Follow me and avoid pain," but "Pick up your cross daily and follow me."

God did not cause this tragedy, in spite of what you might hear from well-meaning friends and from pulpits across this city and this country. I don't pretend to understand God, but since "the Word became flesh and dwelt among us," I know that if I want to know what God is like, I can look to Jesus. During his brief time on earth, Jesus never sent a disease into anyone's body, never blinded anyone, and never killed anyone. But he did heal our diseases, restore sight to the blind, and raise the dead. It's good to know whose side God is on in times like these. I think the fact that God can bring good out of evil has led some to think that God therefore orchestrates evil events that good might result. But there is a surprisingly apt story in Luke's Gospel that will help us avoid making God the author of evil and encourage us to trust that God can bring good even out of this tragedy.

Jesus asks, in Luke 13:4-5: "Or those eighteen who were killed when the tower . . . fell on them—do you think that they were worse offenders than all the others . . . ? No, I tell you; but unless you repent, you will all perish just as they did." Jesus does not get high marks for what we call pastoral care. But do note that he says that this just happened; God

125

didn't knock the tower over to teach people a lesson. Yet Christ insists that we use such a terrible event to take a long, hard look at our own lives and amend our ways—right now. I think of the firefighters and police who ran into the burning towers and toward the pain as others were fleeing. I claim to follow the one who came "not to be served, but to serve"; I claim to admire the one who gave his life as a ransom for many. But am I willing to run toward the pain, to set out to go to the dangerous places, the risky places, in order to meet the needs of others? At a time like this, we need to repent of seeking safety, comfort, and success, and again believe the good news, that those who lose their lives for Christ's sake and the sake of the gospel are the real winners.

Finally, we need to ask ourselves how we will respond as a nation. There is a range of responses open to Christians. They go from a pacifist response, which is part of the Anabaptist and Mennonite tradition, to a just-war response, which is a Christian approach that finds its roots in Saint Augustine in the early fifth century. The pacifist tradition is summed up in the conviction that there are many causes worth dying for, but none worth killing for. The very first cabinet officer to ever resign over a matter of principle was a pacifist Presbyterian Christian. He felt that the president he served was leading us into war. So in 1915, William Jennings Bryan resigned from Woodrow Wilson's cabinet.

At the other end of the spectrum is a just war, which can be broadly summed up as allowing a measured response in order to restore peace, as long as noncombatants are not targeted. That's the continuum. Anything beyond a just war is not a Christian response. Now a Christian might want to get vengeance, or to kill civilians indiscriminately, but that no more makes it an authentically Christian position than a Christian committing adultery makes that a valid option for Christian marriage. For two thousand years, Christians have thought about how to respond to violence against the state. There is no place for vengeance, but only for a desire to stop more violence against the innocent. The reason to go to war against terrorism is not to get revenge, but to restore peace for all.

As we leave today, we can respond by running toward those in need, by running toward the pain in this world and not away from it. We Christians worship a man from the Middle East. This week, we will see many people who are from that part of the world. Let us go to them, speak warmly to them, and let them know we are there for them in their pain of rejection. We can run toward the pain of those in need right here in our own city. We can get involved in meeting their needs by giving our time and talents and money. We need not be passive observers of the world, for we know the power of Christ's resurrection. And more than that, just as he entered into our pain, so we can share in the fellowship of Christ's sufferings by running toward the pain of the world for which Christ died.

Seventeen

Living God's Call

Laura F. Majovski
Pacific Lutheran University

When I hear the question *What does this mean?* I hear, *What does this mean, and what should I do?* Our scripture today reminds us that faith and works go hand in hand (James 2:14-17).

On the one hand, we have a commitment to answer the question *What does this mean?* for Scripture is foundational for our faith. On the other hand, we have a commitment to answer the related question *How then shall I live?*

The Scriptures recount thousands of years of history of God the Creator working to restore and reconcile his creation to himself. For this reason, Jesus came and worked on earth and empowered his disciples. These are tangible expressions of God the Creator working with his creatures toward ultimate eternal restoration. For our part, the Holy Spirit equips us with spiritual gifts to help us do God's work on earth.

For each of us, then, the question is, *How do my spiritual gifts, complemented by my created self, and molded by my life experience, form into my unique self?* And once I know that, *How is my*

self able to further God's kingdom on earth and work for the recon-
ciliation of his creation? Here is where we choose a vocation or
vocational path.

In my case, my spiritual gifts and created self, all molded
by my life experience, led me to choose the vocation of clin-
ical psychologist. My vocational path, if you will, has always
been focused on easing people's pain or life experience so
that they can see God clearly, experience his presence, and
lead the life to which he has called them. So I have worked
in private practice, in psychiatric hospitals, in a university
counseling center, and in university administration. And
with each change of setting, I believe I have answered God's
call to service, always with the same ultimate goal—helping
his creation reconcile with the Creator.

I want to share with you briefly, the stories of three people
who I believe are examples of living that calling wherever
one is. The stories of the first two are told in *The Leadership
Moment,* by Michael Useem, a book that recounts leadership
successes and failures and the lessons to be learned. The
third is from more recent days.

The first is Dr. Roy Vagelos, a distinguished medical
researcher who left a medical faculty position in 1975 to join
one of the nation's leading pharmaceutical firms, Merck. In
the 1980s, he was responsible for product development.
Researchers at Merck had developed Ivomec, which con-
trolled ear mites in cats and heartworms in dogs. It became
the world's leading health care product for animals in the
1980s, and Merck's second biggest moneymaker ever.

A researcher at Merck saw Ivomec's potential for humans,
in particular as a potential cure for a devastating disease—
river blindness. Spread by insects carrying parasites, river
blindness each year affects millions of people in many of the
poorest nations of the world, causing them to lose their sight
permanently.

It was a pivotal moment for Roy and the world. To block
the research for humans might deprive millions of people of

a life with eyesight. But to approve further research might jeopardize corporate profits and shareholders earnings. Even if the drug was effective, the people who needed it could not pay for it. And there was no way to get the drug to them because they lived in the remote parts of the Third World. Fortunately for the world, both Roy's principles and those of the Merck corporation clearly state that health precedes wealth.

He approved continued human research, and ten years later the drug Mectizan was produced, a cure for river blindness. The cost to produce and distribute the drug would be close to $20 million a year before the disease was controlled. The West African victims were too poor to pay for the drug and too isolated to reach easily. No country or foundation wanted to donate the funds, so Roy finally decided to give away the drug to all who need it, forever. He stated "Sometimes in your life, you've got to take a leadership position and make a decision." It was a unique situation in which the drug was needed only by people who couldn't afford it. No matter what the price, the eighteen million people needing the drug were not going to be able to afford it.

(A sidebar: Dr. William H. Foege, executive of the Carter Center and former director of the U.S. Centers for Disease Control, coordinated the distribution of the drug to millions and ended the threat of river blindness. For those who do not recognize the name, he is a class of 1957 PLU alum, living his life of service as a key implementor of world public health.)

Roy was criticized by economists who stated he had violated the stockholders' trust, giving away a product that cost the company $200 million. Roy countered, "We are in the business of preserving and improving human life. All of our actions must be measured by our success in achieving this goal." He noted that not a single shareholder complained about his decision to give the drug away. When asked recently about his fateful decision, he replied that he had no choice but to make the decision. "My whole life has been dedicated to helping people, and this was it for me." Roy Vagelos used his position to bring healing to millions, despite huge financial losses and potential criticism. In his own words: "I had no other choice."

A second example Nancy Barry graduated with her MBA from Harvard and skyrocketed into global banking as an executive at the World Bank, an agency of the United Nations. In 1987 she was one of the bank's five highest-ranking women. She was making decisions on where First World assistance should be spent in Third World projects. If her projects worked well, poor families could start a business and prolong their lives. If her projects failed, the poor stayed trapped in poverty. However, over time, she became doubtful that the World Bank's structure could really meet the needs of the poor.

In early 1990, the tiny rival, Women's World Banking (WWB), asked Nancy if she would consider leading that bank. WWB was dedicated to providing microcredit, or very small $200 loans, for the poor. It was appealing, because she would be the leader of the bank, and it was a small enough corporation to be responsive. If she stayed at World Bank, she would be lending $15 billion annually and leading six thousand employees. At the WWB she would be lending $2 million annually and leading sixty employees. Nancy noted, "If I didn't do it at 40, I never would." It was the moment, she said, to "put my mind and spirit where my mouth was." She left all the power and prestige to lead the tiny WWB. Now, over ten years later, the bank has a goal of reaching one hundred million of the poorest families by 2005. That would add another ninety-two million people to the rolls already receiving small loans to start a business. To Nancy, the connectedness of who we are and what we do is totally related to our effectiveness. Despite her abundant success at the World Bank, it was not the right place for her to work. WWB was. Undergirding her vision of where she is going is an underlying conception of what she should be. Says Nancy: "I believe we were put on Earth for a purpose—for connectedness . . . first to the power that is greater than ourselves," and second, to purpose. Nancy Barry followed a vocational path in banking that allows her to do God's work on earth.

Here's a third example of living God's call wherever one finds oneself. On Tuesday, September 11, a telephone operator was at work on what likely started as a routine day. She assists passengers to make telephone calls from airplanes. At 9:45 A.M., she received a call from a man she'd never met, a passenger on United Flight 93 from Newark to San Francisco. But this would not be like any other call she received before.

Most of us will recognize that fateful date and that fateful flight number. The passenger told her his flight information and that the plane had been hijacked. He asked the operator to call his wife for him. He said, "Please promise that you'll do that for me and let her know how much I love her and the boys." Then he had a second request—for her to pray with him. Together, in that terrifying time, the operator was called upon to recite the Lord's Prayer. In those moments, she went from telephone operator to minister, caring for one of God's created beings in a time of desperate need. They recited the Lord's Prayer together. After he was sure she would talk with his family, he told her that he and some of the other passengers were going to jump one of the hijackers. The next thing she heard was "Let's roll." The phone dropped and she did not hear any more from the passenger.

How did the operator handle that call? She said that in those minutes of talking with the passenger, she felt that she'd made a friend for life. She, a telephone operator, answering a call from an unknown person with a desperate need. She was ready to respond with God's comfort and reassurance in the words of the Lord's Prayer, and later reach out to a grieving family to convey the last words of a loving father and husband.

Three examples—Roy, Nancy, and a telephone operator—three examples of answering the questions *What does this mean?* and *How shall I live?*

All of us, wherever we are, however we spend the hours of the day—either leading a research pharmaceutical company, or a world bank, or working as a telephone operator, or a student, or a faculty or staff member at a university—are called to the same vocation to care for God's creation on earth.

May our faith inspire our works and, however we choose to spend the hours of the day, may our efforts further his kingdom on earth. Amen.

Eighteen

As It Was in the Beginning

William McDonald
Tennessee Wesleyan College

(Psalm 46; Isaiah 2:1-4; Revelation 21:3-4)

The Scriptures spin a long tale of conflict. Didn't it begin with enmity among Adam, Eve, and the serpent? And from there it escalated. A poisoned stream of human wickedness issued forth. Cain murdered Abel. One people became many. Nation rose against nation. Brother against sister. Children against parents. Fractiousness was the result of human sin. A whirlwind of hate covered the earth. Violence became the norm. The world came flying apart as quickly as it had been created.

Those early chapters of Genesis intend to illustrate for us our basic human condition. The world it describes is our world. It's a description for all seasons. The washing represented in the flood episode symbolizes God's commitment to this world, though one washing, of course, would never be enough.

Chapter 12 of Genesis marks a turning point. In the midst of this violent, fractured world, God calls forth the elderly Abraham and Sarah. They are to be the start of a special people. Their lives were to be a story within a story. A story of peace lived out within the world's story of hate. Unlikely people doing extraordinary things; just how unlikely was shown in the fact that these leaders of the new people were a retired herdsman and a woman past menopause. Is that how you begin a new nation?

But these called-out ones were to be the whole world's blessing. Through them God would be present to all people. Without them, the world would cease to exist. They were God's peculiar, chosen people. But the lines between the world and the called-out people were often blurred. They, too, fell into the cycle of sin, hatred, and violence that characterized the rest of the world. In fact, the whole story of the Old Testament can be summed up as a lover's quarrel between God and his people. "You aren't my people. You are my people. You're just like the rest of the world. You are special." This unrelenting tension is the story of Israel.

Israel always knew God's blessing in tangible ways, especially in the presence of children. At every point in the story where it seems like life would not go on, where everything would come to a grinding halt, where the enemy would triumph, life wins. That's why, in Genesis 10, right after the flood, we get a long list of those unpronounceable names. Those long lists come at key points in the story. While we skip over those lists, Hebrew listeners would have cocked their ears. That's just where the promise came: life went on. Children were born. God's promise held.

In fact, the church's chapter of God's people's story begins with just such a list. Into the midst of this unlikely people in this often impossible, crazy world comes another child. Another promise. Another assurance that life will go on, and God's purposes will be worked out through time. This time it was Jesus, who came to be the new Adam. He re-created the world by creating a new people who would announce the kingdom of God. This new community, the church, would not be a nation like Israel, but would bring people together from all nations. The church was to be an international conspiracy against violence, hatred, and blood-shed. Its people followed Jesus, the poet of the Kingdom, the Prince of Peace.

How easy it is to admire Jesus, but how hard to follow him, especially in a time like this. You and I and many of our brothers and sisters in Christ here and around the world are deeply conflicted this morning. I am not immune to emo-tions of rage and revenge. Whoever perpetrated last week's unjustifiable violence should be punished. But I also hear Jesus loud and clear: "Pray for those who persecute you. Bless them that revile you." That's hard to do. It's not what I want to do. Being a Christian is hard. The Ten Command-ments—honor your father and mother; do not murder; do not worship idols—that's the easy stuff. It's Jesus who is so hard to follow. But it is exactly now that our resolve to follow him is tested on so many different levels.

This is exactly the kind of life to which God has called his people throughout the ages, and supremely through Christ. The very peace that Jesus teaches us to pray for is under-mined by my own rage and desire for revenge.

In this complex, fragile, and violent world, we have to think in terms of a big picture. The old Adam and his hatreds must give way to the new Adam and his peace. Just what that means specifically, I don't entirely know. Probably no one does at this point. For starters, I think it might have to do with thinking and acting globally, a willingness to work with others for greater justice around the world. It means defusing violence before it happens, or with doing some-thing about the fact that Americans are 5 percent of the world's people using a third of the world's goods. If you want peace, work for justice. All of those concerns are important. Christians should be concerned about these issues. Yet, all the while, we should remember that our thing is not simply doing more "stuff" to help the world, but living in the world as a people of peace.

Christ's new people are not a nation, but are scattered among and highly influence many nations. Historically, European and American nations have described themselves as Christian. The church cannot be identified with, nor entirely detached from, nations where it has dominated. We must avoid equating any one nation with absolute righteousness, and others with darkness and evil. To do so is to fall into the trap of the possible perpetrators of last Tuesday's evil. The story of every nation and every creed is cast with a mixed bag of saints and sinners, wondrous goodness and damnable evil. Christians, too, have perpetrated our share of evil upon outsiders, in the name of our nations, and in the name of Christ. Christians, and the nations where we live, have sinned and have been sinned against. And all the while, none of it—no violence, no hatred—is justified.

God, be he called "Yahweh" or "Allah," is not pleased with the carnage before us this week past. That's not supposed to be part of the story of Adam, Eve, Abraham, Sarah, Jesus, or Muhammad. But it has become part of the story, our story. It has happened. It can't be edited out.

I shudder to think what words might be clanging from some Christian pulpits this morning. Words about these crimes as some kind of punishment upon this nation—that's exactly what militant fundamentalist Muslims would be hearing, and I'm afraid there's just enough ignorant Christian preaching out there to scare people into submission to such an angry God. Truth is, that's a distortion of both the Christian and the Islamic understanding of God. Neither countenance what has happened. But there are those on both sides who will surely misread their sacred texts. This sort of violence has no place in God's vision for the world. It brings new meaning to describing the banality of evil. God mourns with those who mourn. Our God is the God of the cross whose suffering has made possible the new kingdom aborning in the midst of the old.

I officiated at a wedding yesterday. It was held in a scenic backyard, on a lovely East Tennessee evening. The air was crisp. Children played. The couple was charmed. People ate, laughed, and danced. And yet all of us carried the awful events of the previous Tuesday in our hearts to the wedding feast. We celebrated anyway. At the brink of despair, life triumphed. Death lost. Creation flourished. Human evil wilted.

That wedding is a metaphor for me, a reminder that God has the last word. God's story doesn't end in tears and destruction. It didn't end that way with Jesus, which is why we're here on the first day of the week, resurrection morn. And, the promise is, that it won't end in tears and destruction for the whole world. Near the end of the Bible's story, we have John's vision for a new heaven and a new earth. That's God's vision for the world. That vision is what God's people have been called to be a part of from the beginning. We're called to follow Jesus in making the new out of the old, overcoming evil with good.

Through Jesus alive in us, we are led out of the dizzying cycle of violence and retribution into a completely different way of being. It's a slow process. There are lots of setbacks. In fact, it feels like more setbacks than leaps forward. But, in John's vision, God is calling us into the future, beckoning us toward him. Somehow goodness always wins. Evil never triumphs. It never gets the last word. It never wreaks enough destruction to overcome the final triumph of righteousness. If you believe that, if God's dream for the world is your dream for the world, then you're part of the new community. If you believe it, then beat a sword into a plowshare, and a spear into a pruning hook, and join in God's business of transforming this tired old world into a garden, a place of peace, as it was in the beginning.

Nineteen

Healing for Lives Touched by Violence

Scotty McLennan
Stanford University

Each of us feels, I know, that our lives have been changed dramatically, if not permanently, by the horrendous terrorist violence of last Tuesday. We can't control the feelings that keep coming: grief, anger, fear, sadness and depression, and hopelessness. We want to begin some kind of healing process, but how can we? It's too soon. We don't feel safe. There are so many who have died. So many who have been injured and scarred, physically and emotionally. Some of us have lost family members and close friends. It's likely that all of us will be touched personally over the coming days and weeks as we learn of more and more people, whom we know, who have suffered grievous loss. Our nation will never be the same again, it seems. Our world has forever changed.

On Friday I listened to a Stanford law student, choked with grief, as he spoke about how he'd lost his college roommate on one of the planes that plowed into the World Trade Center. An education school alumnus walked into my office late in the afternoon to tell me about a classmate who died. The classmate had just graduated from the School of Education in June.

I returned home in the evening to receive this email from a colleague at Tufts University, where I worked for sixteen years before coming to Stanford earlier this year: "Scotty, I'm not sure if you have gotten the word, but Janet lost her daughter Mary on American Airlines Flight 11 on Tuesday. Mary was Janet's youngest, and as you probably know, they were inseparable. I hope you didn't have any personal losses amidst this tragedy. God bless."

The Janet my colleague was speaking of—and I've changed her name to protect her confidentiality—was always a wonderful, warm, energetic, optimistic person. Will she ever be the same again?

This is a service of healing for lives touched by violence. How can our Christian faith help us begin the healing process today? For some of us it might come in the powerful music of Fauré's *Requiem* that you'll be hearing throughout the service, or in the hymns we sing together, or in the glorious strains of our organ. For others it may be through prayer or through joining together in the Holy Eucharist. What comfort, though, can we find in this morning's readings from Scripture?

Jesus of Nazareth was a healer, and there are many stories of his healings throughout the New Testament. How did he heal? What did it mean when he healed? How can we be helped, through reading Scripture, to begin our own healing process today?

Let's look at the Gospel lesson: Luke 5:17-26. First of all, we're informed that Jesus was teaching one day, inside a house, surrounded by a huge crowd of people. Some men came—four men, to be precise, as we're told in the same story in the book of Mark—carrying a paralyzed man on a bed. We're not informed how he became paralyzed, but we might well imagine today that it was as a result of violence. No doubt he was physically paralyzed, but we might well imagine ourselves today paralyzed by grief, or fear for our safety, or by depression or hopelessness. The problem,

140

though, was that the four men couldn't maneuver the bed through the crowd and get anywhere near Jesus to ask for healing for their paralyzed friend. But their determination to seek healing was very strong. They managed to get themselves and the bed up onto the roof of the house, they removed a number of tiles, and then they lowered their paralyzed friend on his bed into the middle of the crowd, right in front of Jesus.

When Jesus saw their faith, he told the paralyzed man to stand up and walk, which he did "and went to his home, glorifying God." Please note that the text says that it was because of the four friends' faith that the paralyzed man was healed. Nothing is said about the man's own faith, and Jesus didn't ask him about his religious beliefs, or his background, or whether he was willing to repent for any particular sins. Jesus just healed him on the spot—no questions asked—as a result of those four friends coming together, taking determined action in service to another, and having the faith that their friend could indeed be healed through the grace of God.

In a nutshell, that's the scriptural message for us today, I believe.

Three things are needed for healing to begin for each of us and in this country at large. First, we need to unite in community rather than feel isolated and alone, or in some cases scapegoated and attacked for the color of our skin, our national origin, or our religion. Second, we need to take determined action in service to others, getting up off our haunches, no matter how bad we're feeling, rolling up our sleeves, and going to work to rebuild this country and its confidence. Third, we need to have the faith that God will help those who help themselves; we need to have the faith that healing really is possible if we join with others and get moving.

I have a lot of hope for my friend Janet. She always epitomized those three values of community, service to others, and faith in God. On campus she seemed to be constantly thinking of ways to get people together—to celebrate birthdays and anniversaries, to help people get to know each other from one far-flung segment of the campus to another, and simply to build Tufts's spirit. She thought big and could organize huge events seemingly effortlessly. Besides that she had a great sense of humor and made everyone feel great. She knew the value of community.

In terms of service, I'll never forget one summer when there were terrible drought conditions throughout the Midwest, with lots of farm foreclosures and failing agricultural businesses. Janet started thinking hard about what we could do in Boston. She offered to team up with Catholic Charities and provide housing for members of farming families who would come to Boston to take summer jobs to help get their mothers and fathers, or sisters and brothers, over a very hard stretch.

And Janet always maintained a quiet but deep faith in God. When she left Tufts, she started working with Habitat for Humanity. She told me that what made her happiest about Habitat, besides the community-building and service they provided, was their explicit commitment to seeing themselves as a Christian ministry. One didn't have to be embarrassed to talk about God at work, even as she and the organization were careful to be inclusive of all, regardless of their religious background or lack thereof. Janet had faith that all things are possible with God.

I can think of very little that's worse than losing one's beloved daughter to terrorism last Tuesday. "Mary was Janet's youngest," my colleague wrote, "and as you probably know, they were inseparable." I doubt there'll be any healing possible in Janet's life this Sunday. Yet next week, or next month, or certainly by next year the healing will begin. And it will move into her sinews, and into her bloodstream, and into her heart, and into her very soul. Because I know a community of friends will rally around her in her paralysis. They will lift up the figurative bed on which she is lying, and they will make a determined effort to serve her in whatever way she needs to promote her healing. And since I have an idea of who they are, many of them will act out of their Christian faith that, as the apostle Paul wrote in his epistle to the Romans, "neither death, nor life, nor angels, nor principalities, nor powers, nor things present, nor things to come, nor height, nor depth, nor any other creature, shall be able to separate us from the love of God, which is in Christ Jesus our Lord" (8:38-39 KJV). As the Gospel lesson this morning teaches, it will be by the faith of her friends that Janet's healing progresses.

Yet I actually think that's only part of the story. Because I bet that Janet will soon be out there building community, as she's always done, in response to this national crisis. She'll be comforting others and working to assure that no one is abused because they happen to be Muslim or of Middle Eastern descent. She'll be working to channel her own grief and anger, and that of others, into constructive channels of service rather than into hatred and revenge. And she'll be glorifying and praising God, in whom she lives, and moves, and has her being.

It's contagious, this engagement in community, this service to others, and this faith in God. Healing begins with us, though. The paralyzed man would never have been healed in the Gospel story if four men hadn't come together and taken determined action, founded in faith, to see that their friend was given the opportunity to be healed. We need to come together, as we have here today. We need to commit ourselves to bold and sustained action to build a better world. And we need to share our faith in a loving and just God.

Now, speaking very practically, I have for you some concrete advice, gleaned from various sources over the last week. (It's advice for myself as well, who often finds it rather hard to practice what I preach.)

First, in terms of uniting in community, go to City Hall Plaza in Palo Alto at 5 P.M. for an interfaith, mid-peninsula area-wide prayer service. Don't get glued to your TV for more than half an hour a day, and spend any time saved to be with your roommates and friends, or families or colleagues. Eat with other people whenever you can. Hold at least two people a day and let them know they're not alone.

Second, in terms of taking determined action in service to others, decide whatever it is that you wish to experience and then provide that for another. If you wish to feel that you are safe, for example, cause another to feel that he or she is safe. Make a contribution to the American Red Cross as you leave the church today. Get politically involved, so that you have input into the course of action our nation should take in response to Tuesday's terrorism.

Third, in terms of having faith in God's healing power, remember that all major religions teach the sanctity of human life, and don't let anyone try to justify violence on religious grounds or claim that another religion does so. Take fifteen minutes each morning and fifteen minutes each evening to sit quietly in meditation or prayer; empty yourself of all the noises and images that have cluttered your consciousness this week, and be still with God.

Finally, in the words of the psalmist, "Be strong, and let your heart take courage, all you who hope in the Lord" (Psalm 31:24 NASB).

Twenty

A Chapel Message on Psalm 46

Susan K. Olson
Wesley College, Dover, Delaware

In seminary, I was assigned a sermon on Psalm 46 as my final exam for a preaching class. I returned it by mail, in an envelope postmarked January 2, 1992.

Now, January 2, 1992, was a lifetime ago. Most of you students were still in Garanimals® then. I pulled out that old sermon, never preached, when the words of Psalm 46 could not leave my head this week. I wondered if there was anything in it worth salvaging.

The truth is, there wasn't much.

The sermon was written from my parent's cozy home. I was well and happy. Every military action that had occurred in my life had happened somewhere "over there," wherever "there" is.

This isn't over there. This is here. This is in buildings that I have been in and on airlines that I have flown. This is in airports that I have checked through. This is, most likely, at least somebody I have met. And even if it isn't somebody I have met or buildings I have been in, this is my home. This is your home, your New York, your Washington, your Pennsylvania, your Dulles, your Newark, your Boston.

And, if you are at all like me, this is the scariest, largest collective experience that you have ever had. I wasn't alive when Kennedy was shot. I wasn't alive for Pearl Harbor. I was alive for the *Challenger* explosion, but that was somehow different. As tragic as it was, we knew that there was a danger implicit in that endeavor. Nobody ever thought it would be dangerous to go to work on a Tuesday morning. Nobody.

A friend of mine is a peacekeeper for the Presbyterian Church. His job is to go to countries after wars and help them to hold elections, to appoint judges, to rebuild governments. He has been in virtually every war-torn country. Currently, he lives in New York City. The day after the World Trade Center fell, he wrote this: "New York was bombed today. While using commercial airliners has its own twisted horror, these planes were bombs—transcontinental flights loaded with fuel, the largest explosive devices that the perpetrators could get their hands on to destroy their targets. We are suddenly facing the horrors of bombardment that people in so many other places have faced—Sarajevo, Jerusalem, Ramallah, Baghdad, Belgrade, Belfast, Freetown, and on and on . . . suddenly sharing a terror and vulnerability that was unknown to us, as we are very used to feeling safe and secure from attack. But acts of war reached us today. I have seen its aftermath in too many places; this is a first, to be in the midst of it."

I don't know if they have the same rides at amusement parks now as they used to, but does anyone remember the one where they loaded all of us kids into this barrel and then spun us around and around until we were going really fast? If you remember it, you remember what happens next: the floor would drop out, and we'd be pinned to the wall—by centrifugal force or some other science word—just pinned to the sides of this colossal barrel, with our feet having nothing to rest on.

I am not a fan of amusement parks, and that ride is partly to blame. I remember, still, that flip in the stomach when you realize that the floor—the solid thing that you trust to hold you up—is gone. I remember that feeling, because I experienced it again last Tuesday . . . and Wednesday . . . and Thursday . . .

So when everything that you've ever trusted in falls out, and the floor is gone, and your feet are dangling in midair, what do you do? Where do you go? What do you believe? In whom do you find your confidence? Where in the Bible do you even find comfort?

Personally, I vote for the psalms. John Calvin, in his commentary on Psalms written in 1563, said that he could truly call the book of Psalms an anatomy of all parts of the soul. The psalms mirror the emotions in the souls of men and women.

Psalm 46 is a psalm of confidence. We don't really know for sure why it was written. There are several good theories, but the common theme is that it was absolutely written during a time of national crisis. The entire psalm is in the plural. God is *our* refuge and *our* strength. This isn't the psalm of a hurting soul. It is the psalm of a hurting world. This is the psalm of people who can see the nations in an uproar, and the kingdoms tottering. This is the psalm of people who can see the earth change, and the mountains shake in the heart of the sea. We can see the waters roar and foam and the mountains tremble with tumult. The psalmist sees the airplanes soar into buildings, and the carnage and smoke, and yet, says, "God is our refuge and strength."

A refuge, according to the *American Heritage* dictionary, is a "protection or shelter, as from danger or hardship; something to which one may turn for help or relief; a place providing protection or shelter; a haven."

A haven. A safe dwelling place. A secure abode. A sanctuary. God is our haven, our secure place. It's almost as if we could crawl into the safety of God, like a frightened child crawls into a parent's arms.

147

God is our refuge *and* our strength. God offers us not just the security of a haven, but the refortitude to go back into the world to face our fears with God's strength as our own. Accepting God's refuge is not a way out for cowards. Indeed, God's refuge supplies us also with the strength to carry on, even when we think we are on our own. Not unlike a parent's firm hand on the back of a seven-year-old's wobbly bicycle, God provides us with what we need in support, while still making us pedal our own bicycle.

Like my friend said, I'm used to feeling secure in my own country. I don't like feeling sad and nervous. But I can't let that stop me. This weekend a small group of us are headed to D.C. to do service work. I'm a little nervous about being in the nation's capital so soon after the attack, but I know that with God as our refuge and our strength, we will not be alone. God can and does provide us with both the refuge (the hiding place) and the strength (the fortitude and encouragement) to face all that the world has to give us.

The question that has been asked all week is, How could God let this happen? I don't know. Billy Graham doesn't know. The pope doesn't know. My favorite seminary professor doesn't know. I don't know.

What I do know is this: the God of refuge loves us and does not wish this evil upon us. The God of refuge and strength gave every last dying soul on those planes and in those buildings a place of refuge in their last minutes, and that same God holds them all in loving arms today. Elie Wiesel, a Holocaust survivor and scholar wrote this: "God accompanies his children into exile. . . . No space is devoid of God. God is everywhere, even in suffering. . . . What happens to us touches God." I know this to be true. God was on those planes, and in those buildings. God was with the firefighters and police officers. God was there. God is there.

I said this to a friend, too. His response: "But how do you know that?"

I just believe it. And if faith is the assurance of things hoped for and the conviction of things not seen, then that is enough.

An unknown Jewish person—we don't even know if the person was a man or woman—left perhaps the greatest testament to faith behind on the wall of a cellar where Jews hid from Nazi forces in Cologne, Germany. And though you have already seen the words, I'll say them again, for they bear repeating in this day of tumult, where mountains shake and waters roar and foam.

I believe in the sun, even when it isn't shining.
I believe in love, even when there's no one there.
And I believe in God, I believe in God, even when God is silent.

May we all live with such confidence in the God of refuge and strength.

Amen.

Twenty-one

A Sermon Preached at University Presbyterian Church

Earl F. Palmer
Seattle, Washington

The week of September 11, 2001, has imprinted upon our minds and hearts pictures and sounds we will never forget. The raw evil of terrorism attacked our country, took away precious lives, and left thousands of others as casualties of these brutal acts: people physically wounded, families who lost a father or mother, sister or brother.

We in Seattle are many miles from Washington, D.C., Pennsylvania, and New York City, but we experienced that day as we and all the world watched and listened, and prayed and waited. We witnessed tragedy, and we also witnessed the sheer courage of firefighters, police officers, and ordinary office workers who helped wounded people find safety. We will never forget the courage of New York's firefighters who entered a stricken building to help find people. They have enriched the meaning of the word *hero*. Now it is the task of every civilized nation to work together to find and bring to justice the terrorists who planned this assault on human life.

As your pastor, I have been asking the questions, *What can we do as a congregation in Seattle to be helpful to those who have endured so much harm? What can we do to minister thoughtfully to our people here in our congregation and in this city?*

First, we pray for God's help. We are a worshiping fellowship; and on the evening of September 11, a large gathering of our people met at UPC to pray. On Friday, September 14, at noon, we mourned and prayed in public worship for those who died; and we thanked God for the bravery and love that was shown by the heroes of that day. On today, September 16, we are worshiping, the Sunday school is loving our children, we will listen to God's word, and we will pray for peace and hope. We are also receiving a special offering to aid those who suffered in this disaster; we pray for the safety of our Muslim neighbors and for the protection of those of Middle Eastern heritage in our country.

Second, we as a church must carry on with the mandate of the gospel and invest in the future with hope and thoughtful strategy. On Sunday, September 9, we commissioned our Sunday school teachers; and today, we commission an outstanding group of young university graduates who will be in ministry this year as interns among our youth and university students. On October 21, we will present our fourth-graders with their Bibles. Our task is clear: we must, with the help of God's grace, show his love and teach the truth of the gospel. We must not retreat from this good responsibility, because the best cure for the bad is the healthy diet of the good.

Third, our Children and Family Ministries has prepared a very helpful packet of guidance information to aid parents in comforting children during times of crises. These packets are available at the church.

Fourth, each of us in our families needs to reach out toward one another. We need our neighbors, we need to feel safe with each other, and we need to be washed and comforted by the love that heals. We need to learn the truth of the good news, and to know the joy that comes from the Lord of Peace.

151

Our message for today is the second in a series of expositional sermons on the Teacher, Jesus of Nazareth, and his Sermon on the Mount. Matthew narrates this sermon in three chapters: 5, 6, and 7. Last Sunday, we listened in on this sermon as Jesus shared nine blessings. Today we look at a bold sentence (by our Teacher) that follows those blessings that we call the Beatitudes:

> "Do not think that I have come to abolish the law or the prophets; I have come not to abolish but to fulfill. For truly I tell you, until heaven and earth pass away, not one letter, not one stroke of a letter, will pass from the law until all is accomplished." (Matthew 5:17-18)

With this sentence, Jesus takes into his hands the Law of Moses, and the Prophets of sacred Scripture. At this point Jesus could conceivably move in several directions in his sermon. He could *reject* everything in the people's past: their traditions and their law. Some few listeners might have welcomed just that sort of approach. After all, even with the possession of the Law of Moses, and the traditions that grew out of the Law, as a people, they were apparently little better off under Roman oppression than during the time when they first received the Torah more than twelve hundred years earlier in the wilderness. When some people feel that kind of social and political helplessness, they often welcome prophets who throw out the past, with its apparent impotence, and offer what appears to be a totally new option. In his *Letters and Papers from Prison,* Dietrich Bonhoeffer described this mood and desire as those who want a "fruitful radicalism in the place of a barren mediocrity." Could it not have been argued that the law of Mount Sinai had failed, along with the prophets who honored the Law?

Another group who might have welcomed the discarding of the Law were those who felt personally trapped and demoralized by it. The Law represented condemnation to them because they felt its weight upon their shoulders, and if Jesus were to cancel it, he would probably have had their support. If we feel condemned by the Law because of certain of our sins, we might welcome the elimination of the document that makes us feel guilty.

Jesus could also take the opposite approach; he could simply and plainly *restate* the Law as the common tradition of the people. He might join the Sadducees and return strictly to the texts of the Pentateuch, or he might include the broader way of the Pharisees, whose later traditions of interpretation had been refined since the time of the Maccabean Revolt (about 160 B.C.). If Jesus were to favor the more limited way, he would have the support of the Sadducee party; if he were to favor the broader restatement, he would have the support of the Pharisee party.

Jesus chooses a third way, and risks the disappointment of all the special interest groups now waiting to hear his teaching. He takes hold of the Law and the traditions that surround the Ten Commandments as if they were an unfinished portrait; he now draws together the separate parts of the Law toward the completion of their original intention. Think of it this way; Jesus treats the Law as if it were a great arc.

Have you ever put together an electric train? Four years ago my grownup kids gave me a Lionel train because I always wanted one and they knew it. I put it together, and its oval track surrounds our Christmas tree each Christmas. Did you ever look at one of the curved sections of track? It just seems to cry out for more track; and if you keep adding other curved sections, it will make a perfect circle. Add some straight track, and you have an oval. The curve is a perfect arc, and it anticipates its completion as a circle. It has meaning and integrity within itself, but it wants its fulfillment.

Jesus now extends the line of the arc around to its fulfillment, the circle for which it was originally designed. Jesus completes the circle, and that is the meaning of the word that he uses to describe his purpose toward the Law and the

153

Prophets: *fulfill. Fulfill* means literally to "fill up or complete." C. S. Lewis explains this unforgettably in his book *Miracles:*

> Let us suppose we possess parts of a novel or a symphony. Someone now brings us a newly discovered piece of manuscript and says, "This is the missing part of the work. This is the chapter on which the whole plot of the novel really turned. This is the main theme of the symphony." Our business would be to see whether the new passage, if admitted to the central place which the discoverer claimed for it, did actually illuminate all the parts we had already seen and "pull them together." Nor should we be likely to go very far wrong. The new passage, if spurious, however attractive it looked at the first glance, would become harder and harder to reconcile with the rest of the work the longer we considered the matter. But if it were genuine, then at every fresh hearing of the music or every fresh reading of the book, we should find it settling down, making itself more at home, and eliciting significance from all sorts of details in the whole work which we had hitherto neglected.[1]

The prophets of the Bible preached and lived out three messages as they spoke for God on the importance of righteousness:

1. First was the ethical theme in every prophet's affirmation, with its clear call to repentance by the people.
2. The prophets also announced stern judgment themes, as in Isaiah 1, where the Lord says to the people through Isaiah that the Lord cannot be with their solemn assemblies because they have blood on their hands. Jeremiah speaks this stern judgment for God to the people by saying that their hurt is incurable.
3. Ironically, the words of hope are usually right next to the judgment sentences. Following Isaiah's harsh warning that the Lord will not endure us because of our

bloodied hands comes the sentence "Come now, and let us reason together, says the Lord. Though your sins are as scarlet, they shall be as white as snow" (Isaiah 1:18 NASB).

Also, Jeremiah's greatest promise follows as the next sentence. After the harsh words of our incurable illness, the words we heard in today's Old Testament lesson: "I will restore your health. . . ." These prophetic words of judgment and hope converge at the profound events at Mount Calvary and the empty tomb of Easter.

I remember an unforgettable experience of mine when I was a young pastor here at UPC. Karl Barth made his one trip to America in 1963 and gave a series of lectures at Princeton, which I was fortunate to attend. On one evening, in the Princeton Lounge, he answered questions from the more than one thousand students and theologians who were present. The questions were translated to him in German, and then Barth answered them in English. A few weeks earlier, Nazi war criminal SS Officer Adolf Eichmann had been captured and was then on trial for his crimes against humanity. One student asked, "Dr. Barth, now that Adolf Eichmann has been caught, can we now put the guilt of Germany on his shoulders?" There was an electricity in the air as we waited for the answer from this great theologian, who had bravely opposed Hitler; who had written the Barmen Declaration in 1934; who had been expelled from Germany and his teaching post at Bonn; and who then as a Swiss theologian took up what became his lifelong post at Basel University. Barth spoke: "No, the guilt of Germany has been placed on quite another man's shoulders."

I will never forget that moment; it was the sheer breakthrough of the gospel in that room. Jesus Christ is the only one able to fulfill the Prophets, with their complicated three-part message of righteousness, severe judgment, and hope for God's Messiah. It has all come together on the shoulders

155

of one man—Jesus Christ. He has taken our place at the cross of Calvary, where he has defeated sin and death and the power of all evil, including the devil, by disarming them of their final power. Jesus will bring the arc of the Prophets' message around to its grand fulfillment. The disciples hear of that fulfillment in our Lord's Sermon, and they will experience that fulfillment as events on Holy Friday and Holy Sunday.

This week, two Christian television preachers made the statement that, in their view, the tragedy at New York City's World Trade Center had perhaps happened because God had withdrawn his protection from America in judgment because of our national sinfulness. Our president called their remarks unhelpful and hurtful. I agree with the president; but, as a Christian, I must challenge their words at an even deeper level. Their words are false teaching. What they said reveals a faulty Christology. It was Karl Barth who said, "Tell me how it stands with your Christology and I will tell you who you are." Jesus Christ, in himself, has fulfilled the Prophets' stern warning as much as their hopes for God's salvation. This Jesus is the one who boundaries the whole of human history. The fact is that only once did God withdraw his protective boundary, and that was when his Son, Jesus, was alone on the cross.

There is a mystery also in human history; because one of God's sovereign decisions is the decision that gives us real freedom, which means we can do good or we can do harm. Therefore, within the grand boundaries of our creation by God's decision, and the final fulfilling of history in the return of Jesus Christ, the line of our human story is turbulent. There are the brilliant strokes of human goodness and wisdom with the positive consequences that result. But there are also the downward strokes of human evil and cruelty; acts which are against the will of God. Therefore tragedy is concrete and real; but even our acts that do harm are not ultimate, because Jesus Christ holds in his hand the boundary. Not only that, but his faithfulness and grace are able to redeem in the middle of tragedy.

At the national worship service, America's beloved pastor, the Reverend Billy Graham, said it simply and powerfully. He tenderly spoke to our country in its time of grief, and his deepest word of comfort came when he said there is a mystery about evil, but that he, as a Christian, looks to the person Jesus Christ, who endured all evil on the cross; Jesus understands our tragedy and he has conquered death itself. As Billy Graham spoke, the TV camera in that great National Cathedral lifted and focused on the cross of Christ on the altar of the church.

We have a man for the crisis who is better than a theory or a set of answers; the man who has fulfilled every judgment and every hope of the prophets. Let us hear Jesus, that man, speak to us as he did on the Thursday evening of Holy Week:

> "I will not leave you desolate; I will come to you. Yet a little while, and the world will see me no more, but you will see me; because I live, you will live also. . . . Peace I leave with you; my peace I give to you. . . . Let not your hearts be troubled, neither let them be afraid. . . . I have said this to you, that in me you may have peace. In the world you have tribulation; but be of good cheer, I have overcome the world." (John 14:18, 19, 27; 16:33 RSV)

Note

1. C. S. Lewis, *Miracles: A Preliminary Study* (New York: Macmillan, 1947), pp. 132-33.

Twenty-two

A Sermon

Joerg Rieger
Perkins Chapel
Southern Methodist University

(Psalm 130; 1 Corinthians 12:12-26)

At the beginning of theology classes, I often tell my students that theology is a matter of life and death. Some of you may have thought that I was just making this up. But here we go.

A Day of Death

Yesterday was a day of death. Thousands of people died in New York City; in Arlington, Virginia; and in a plane crash in Pennsylvania. We don't know exactly how many are dead. The first question of my six-year-old twin daughters was whether there were children among them. "Yes," I told them, "most likely there are children among the people who died."

Someone on TV last night stated the obvious: this event is part of us. There is no doubt that the pain experienced on the East Coast is shared throughout the whole country. My parents called from Germany and shared their concerns. Friends emailed from places as far away as Zimbabwe. Many others around the world share this pain with us. Saint Paul realized long ago that "when one member suffers, all suffer together with it."

I do not expect any visitors who will come to my office after this service and tell me that yesterday's events are only a matter of the special interests of those who died and their families. We all know that yesterday was *our* day of death.

Yesterday was a day of death. Yesterday, thousands of children around the world also died from hunger and preventable causes. The United Nations tells us that the number of children who died yesterday is around thirty thousand. Thirty thousand more children will be dead when this day is over. Yet many people assume that the death of these children is a matter of special interest. You need to know about these dead children only if you happen to be concerned with international social issues, with the so-called "third world," or if you somehow happen to be some kind of liberation theologian. Here is a common reaction: "Yea, yea, Rieger is talking about the 'third world' again." But remember Saint Paul: "When one member suffers, all suffer together with it."

Yesterday was *our* day of death. The death of so many of our fellow Americans might serve as a wake-up call. People are dying all around us. The many thousands that died in the terrorist attacks are joined by thirty thousand children. They are joined by many of our young African American brothers in this country whose life expectancy on average is much lower than that of the rest of America. And they are joined by a record number of deaths of Hispanic workers on our construction sites in Texas, as reported by the *Dallas Morning News* on Sunday (September 9, 2001). The thousands who died yesterday are also joined by battered women and children who sometimes don't make it. "When one member suffers, all suffer together with it." No more special interests when it comes to suffering. These events are also part of us.

159

Theology of Death

Yesterday was *our* day of death. But what does theology have to do with all of these tragedies? There is a theology of death that accompanies these events. This theology of death suggests that we can change the world through violence, that we need bombs and airplanes and missiles to assure that our will be done. The theology of death also suggests that what happens to those who are not members of our own national or ethnic groups does not matter. For some, this means that killing those who are not part of one's group is all right. For others, this means that we don't need to pay attention when people around the world are dying.

There is a theology of death that suggests that we have a right to push our own advantage, regardless. It suggests that we can do whatever suits us, without concern for other people's lives. The theology of death expects death to continue. And so tomorrow will be another day of death. And there will be another day of death after that. Don't think that those who committed the terrorist attacks yesterday will be surprised by revenge and repercussions. They fully expect that this will happen. And they will be back, also revenging. This is the circle of violence in which a theology of death thrives.

Yesterday was a day of death. Nobody doubts that yesterday will go down in history, together with Pearl Harbor and other national catastrophes. Has it ever occurred to you that, together with this atrocious event, the daily deaths of thirty thousand children will also go down in history? One day our children and grandchildren will ask us about these deaths as well. And they will confront us with our own theology of death that fully expects death to continue.

Theology of Life

What we really need in the midst of all this death and dying is a theology of life. A theology of life needs to begin

160

with an account of death. What causes people to die? What are the principalities and powers that kill? We need to get to the bottom of the powers of death and realize how all of us are easily pulled into vicious circles of violence.

But a theology of life affirms that death does not have the last word. As Christians, we believe that Jesus Christ—who also was killed in a vicious circle of violence—has overcome the powers of death. Christ's resurrection offers new hope. A theology of life is rooted in the resurrection as a response to unjust death.

But make no mistake. In the midst of death, a theology of life does not come easy. If you think that all you need is a few pious statements, you have not yet encountered the scary powers of death. The events on the East Coast yesterday have shaken us up because they remind us of the potential threat to our own life. This experience brings us closer to the experience of many people around the world who fear for their lives on a daily basis. What is our worst nightmare is a daily reality for many people around the globe. Don't forget the children.

To make things even more complicated, both a theology of death and a theology of life may sound perfectly orthodox. Both will probably confess with the tradition of the church that "Jesus Christ is Lord." But what they mean by that is different. Does Christ's lordship equal a reign of violence, bombs, missile attacks, and economic superiority? Or does Christ's lordship have to do with sharing the pain of those who suffer, with comforting the victims, and with working for a new world where violence is no longer the answer?

In the resurrection, Christ goes ahead of us on the way that leads to life, together with all the dead and the dying. Christ makes a way where there was no way before. This is what guides us into a theology of life. The question at this point is not so much, "What would Jesus do?" but, "What is Jesus doing now?" Where is Jesus walking the streets of this world right now? What about New York City? What about

Dallas and every other place in this country, and on every continent? Here lies our hope. But here is the challenge as well: if we begin to walk together with Jesus in the company of the dead, we might find that we need to walk a different walk. We will be walking where there seemed to be no way at all.

Yesterday was a day of death. As we conclude this service with the celebration of Holy Communion, I want to invite you to join me on the journey toward a theology of life. I invite you to pay attention. You will find glimpses of the theology of life in the liturgy that follows. You will find glimpses of the theology of life also in the music and hymns. And I trust that we will find glimpses of a theology of life also in each other as we share in the celebration of communion with all of God's people all over the world, dead or alive.

Amen.

Twenty-three

In the Presence of the Enemy

Elizabeth McGregor Simmons
University Presbyterian Church
San Antonio, Texas

(Psalm 23; Luke 15:1-10)

When the events of Tuesday occurred, immediately the question presented itself: Should we scrap the lectionary text for the day and the music that had been chosen to partner with the sermon in proclaiming its message? Should we find another Scripture passage, a different anthem and hymns, that seem to address the situation more directly? We wrestled with this, but ultimately, it seemed, to go poking around the Bible and the music library for something that would merely mirror our own feelings and opinions would be to limit what the Spirit might have to say to this congregation today.

What I had not anticipated, but what has happened for me personally, is that in sticking with the Gospel lesson prescribed by the lectionary, I have felt drawn into a large community, the community of ministers and priests across the country and indeed around the world; all of us reading the same Scripture passage, all of us grasping for a faithful word to speak to the congregations we serve in the face of this unspeakable horror. Knowing that we here at University

Presbyterian Church are reading and reflecting upon Jesus' parables of the lost coin and the lost sheep in unison with Christian congregations in many places today is a powerful thing for me to consider, and I hope for you as well.

A picture is worth a thousand words, it is said, and never has this been more true than it has been this week.

While thousands and thousands of words have glutted the airwaves, it is the pictures, the images, that have been deposited permanently in our memory banks. The image of the jetliner plowing into the World Trade Center, and the grotesque flames of the impact. The image of rescue workers, their faces creased with weariness, digging res-olutely through rubble. The image of firefighters planting an American flag, caught by a New Jersey photojournalist, in a pose movingly reminiscent of the combatants at Iwo Jima. The image which brought a lump to my throat that took ever so long to dissolve—the sight of the red-coated British guards playing "The Star-Spangled Banner" at Buckingham Palace for the first time ever, at the order of the queen.

A picture is worth a thousand words, it is said. Thus the most powerful teaching that Jesus did while he was on earth was accomplished through the images that he projected onto the screens of his hearers' minds in the form of para-bles. In the two familiar parables that we have read today, two strong images emerge: that of a shepherd, his face creased with weariness, searching the wilderness resolutely for one lost sheep; and that of a woman, her face creased with weariness, lighting a lamp and searching every corner of her house resolutely for one lost coin.

To us they seem to be gentle images, exuding warmth and loving care. In fact, one of the Bibles that line my shelves has a note attached to these parables. "Severe and Gentle Stories," it is titled, and goes on to suggest that in Luke 14, there are harsh stories that are intended to be severe warn-ings; but here in Luke 15, Jesus folds his frame into a rocking chair, lifts his audience up into his lap, softens his voice, and reads them a gentle, loving bedtime story.

Gentle the parables of the lost sheep and the lost coin may seem as they fall upon our modern-day ears. However, to the ears of the folk to whom Jesus uttered them originally, these images—the image of a shepherd, the image of a woman— were as jarring, harsh, and offensive and disgusting as images of planes smashing into skyscrapers are to us.

For, you see, the good religious folk to whom Jesus told these stories had this way of looking at the world and at other people in a way that made sense to them. The way they saw it, there were "sinners" and us; "enemies" and us, "them" and us. And included in that "sinner/enemy/them" category were shepherds and women. Shepherds because they had their hands all over sheep all day long, sheep dung under their fingernails and sheep smell permanently clinging to their T-shirts, and, in the religious leaders' religiously neatnik minds, that meant that shepherds could never get quite clean enough to venture any farther into God's house than, say, the back porch. Women because, well, they're not all that clean either; you know that icky thing that happens to them once a month, and they always have baby spit-up on them, and isn't that reason enough to fall down on your knees with the others at the Tuesday morning men's Bible study, lift your face to heaven, and pray, "Thank you, God, that you did not create me a woman" (which is exactly what they prayed back in those days).

That was the religious leaders' image of how things were. Shepherds/Us. Women/Us. Sinners-Enemies-Them/Us. That was the religious leaders' image of how things were, but it wasn't Jesus' image of how things really are. What Jesus told those religious leaders was this: That shepherd that you consider unclean, God looks a lot like him, going out to whatever wilderness where the sheep has been lost and persevering to bring it back to the sheepfold and into the community of the other sheep. That woman you thank God that you're not, God looks a lot like her, holding up a candle to shine light into every corner of the room so that no coin, no person, remains trapped, isolated, and lost in a dark place.

These are the images Jesus used to describe God, and, by implication, if we consider ourselves to be created in the image of God, they are the images that ought to guide the way that we live, too. The images in these two parables in Luke 15 call us to be shepherds, to be light-bearing women, who give the whole of ourselves to the work of bringing people back into community with one another.

These images, as strong as they are, are going to be difficult for people of faith, such as we claim to be, to cling to in the days ahead, I imagine. There will be much to wrench these images from our minds and hearts and tempt us to lapse back into that Sinners/Us, Enemy/Us, Them/Us way of thinking.

Some of those who will try to wrench those images from us will be people with whom we live and work and go to school.

Over the past few days, there has been much written and said about violence and the possibility of violence against persons who are Muslim or of Arab descent. It has already happened right down the street. It has already happened to a young man of Arab descent who has been subjected to harassment while in juvenile detention. In all likelihood, there is not a person here who does not find that kind of violence reprehensible. But while we would never pepper a restaurant owned by Arab Americans with rocks or bullets, what will we do when a week from now or a month from now we're pouring a cup of coffee in the break room at work, and one of our coworkers walks up and says, "Hey, did you hear the one about the Muslim who . . . ?"

Or what we will do if we're sitting in a classroom and the principal breaks in with an announcement over the intercom saying that missiles are sailing into Afghanistan, and the whole class erupts in a cheer?

I've been thinking a lot about that one. I've been thinking

a lot about those of you who spend a good part of every weekday in high school or elementary school. I suspect that you may be facing the greatest challenge of all of us, and here is why I think that:

One November day, I was sitting in Mr. Smith's sixth-grade class. I don't recall what we had just finished doing or what we were about to do; all I remember is that Mr. Smith had left the room momentarily, and then he quickly returned, his lips parted in a broad grin. Instead of telling us that we were getting an extra-long recess, he said, "President Kennedy has been shot." In a single instant, the boy with the blond buzz haircut sitting next to me leaned over and said, "Well, the n____ lover got what was coming to him," and the whole class erupted in one long, sustained, and what to my ears sounded like a unanimous cheer.

Does that sound hard to believe? Well, I'll tell you something that is even harder to believe. In the midst of all the cheering and racist remarks, I said nothing. As wrong as I knew what was happening in that room to be, I sat there and said nothing. I didn't challenge my teacher; he had the power to lower my grade, after all. I didn't challenge my friends; as mistaken as they may have been, they weren't terrible people as individuals, I knew, and if I challenged them, what would they say about me? So I sat there, and I said nothing.

Until today.

Today, I challenge those of you who may sit in a similar place to where I sat on that long ago November day to do better than I did. Cling to the images that Jesus gave us of a God who embraces all of the sheep, and of a woman who shines her light into every nook of darkness; claim these as the very images in which you yourself were created. And when your classmates cheer or your teacher grins, challenge them by saying something like, "Whether or not you believe that war is necessary, please do not cheer, for war is never a good thing. It is a terrible, terrible thing. People will be hurt;

people will be killed in war—our sisters and brothers in the military; children and families in Afghanistan and other countries, perhaps even in our own; all of these, every one of them as precious to God as you yourself are. So please do not cheer; grieve. Grieve as God does whenever God's children break community and are at war with one another, and throw yourself into the work of creating a world where prejudice, oppression, and war are no more."

A picture is worth a thousand words, it is said, and, in the living of these days, let us pray that our God will keep the pictures of our loving-shepherd God and our light-bearing woman God ever before us and engrave these images indelibly upon our thinking, our speaking, and our acting.

Twenty-four

A Christian Patriot's Dream: Seeing Beyond the Tears and Humiliation of Mass Violence

Frederick J. Streets
Battell Chapel, Yale University

(Psalm 139:1-18, 22-23; Matthew 5:1-9; Romans 8:35, 37-39)

> "Blessed are the peacemakers, for they will be called children of God." (Matthew 5:9)

> "The LORD is my light and salvation; whom shall I fear? The LORD is the stronghold of my life; of whom shall I be afraid?" (Psalm 27:1)

I, like all of you, am searching for the words to express my thoughts and feelings about the terrorists' attack and murder of people in New York, Pennsylvania, and Washington, D.C., this past Tuesday. For a long time to come we will need the help of those among us who are teachers, artists, musicians, poets, writers, and preachers of all kinds to voice our sorrow, longings, and hope. We will need to listen to one another, especially to those who escaped, and those who were injured, and all who lost loved ones and friends.

It is important that we create and take advantage of opportunities to talk and reflect, to be in silence, alone or with others in our effort to cope with our national sense of having been violated, and take from this experience a greater capacity to build a better, not bitter, America.

So we have gathered to pray, listen to scriptures read and other words spoken, and music played. Most important, we come before God, and to offer our presence to one another and draw from our vulnerability a sense of comfort, and from our faith strength and hope.

In a crisis we rely upon what we know and return as soon as possible to our familiar pattern of life. We use these as anchors. However, they will not be enough for us to move forward with confidence and a sense of security while facing the evil wind that has blown upon America. It will take time for us to learn from this national tragedy what it is we will need to know in order to adjust and create a new vision of our society and global relationships. These are some of the many challenges thrust upon us by last Tuesday's events. There are others.

In the midst of our prosperity and the promise of our struggle to become a more multicultural and inclusive society, we must now turn our attention, energy, and resources to identify, develop, and implement a strategy to fight an external enemy. How can we do this and continue to improve our common quality of life? How will our possible use of $40 billion for defense affect, for example, public education, our programs of health care, and social welfare?

What kind of society will we allow ourselves to become as a result of our having been attacked? We must not allow our appropriate rise in patriotism to lead us into a blinding nationalism, unwilling to be self-critical or seek to understand the ways other people in the world see this nation, nor should we have an attitude of religious imperialism that makes those our enemy whose ethnicity, religious beliefs, skin color, or sexual orientation are different from our own. Earlier this week, after sharing this perspective in a speech at a community service in a neighboring town, a woman came up to me and told me that I was doing the work of the anti-Christ. She felt that Tuesday's bombings were a sign from God of God's wrath upon America and the need for all Americans to confess Jesus as their Lord and Savior.

A Muslim student being interviewed on television this week said he wished that he could become invisible because of his fear that he would be attacked because he was a Muslim. I have an idea of what he meant. I know what it feels like to be objectified, made to feel like a "thing"—to be the focus of someone's unwarranted hatred.

I think that one of the spiritual opportunities afforded to us by the crisis we now face is our recognition of our common humanity and fundamental equality as human beings. This can have a deep and profound impact upon and transform our civil and global society.

God cannot be the scapegoat and held responsible for the actions of the terrorists on Tuesday. We have free will to inflict harm or show love toward other people. There needs to be global discussion on what motivates us to do evil and what is needed to diminish it as attractive and preferential.

I am, as many of you know, a member of the Harvard Program in Refugee Trauma, founded by Dr. Richard Mollica, who is a psychiatrist and graduate of Yale Divinity School. As a member of this team, I have been working with members of the clergy, and medical and mental health professions in Bosnia. I want to share with you some of the things we have learned over the years in working with victims and survivors of mass violence, war, and torture.

The surreal nature of what happened to our nation and world has given way to the reality of the evil inflicted upon us. The horrible images of last Tuesday that all of us have seen join the litany of modern atrocities of the unspeakable horror associated with mass violence in our modern time. We now share with millions of people abroad the experience and painful knowledge that at the core of modern mass violence is the aim to humiliate its victims.

Mass violence in all of its forms of torture and terrorism is aimed at humiliating individuals, their community, society, and nation. Those who designed means of mass violence want to humiliate their victims so deeply that their entire culture and way of life are annihilated, or at the least, radically transformed. The terrorists who attacked our great symbols of American society know that although they could not destroy America, they could deeply humiliate all of us and possibly break our spirits.

Unfortunately, we are limited in our interpretations of the aims of mass violence, and methods to prevent them and heal its victims. The humiliation of mass violence leaves within the survivors a scar so deep that its damaging effects extend well beyond the life of the person affected.

The disappearance and death of those thousands in the World Trade Center will continue to haunt their families into the next generation. I have seen this effect of mass violence on some of the people with whom I worked and know in Bosnia and Colombia and met in a refugee camp in Ghana, West Africa. The world has witnessed the same thing happen to people in Argentina and Chile.

The threat to the health of those who survive, their family members, and rescuers is a major concern. They will need people to listen to their experiences and to help them deal with their fears. A gap is created between those who were directly exposed to terror and violence, and those who were not. Those directly harmed may feel humiliated, ashamed, and alienated from society. Solidarity and the outpouring of generosity, support, and real affection toward them that is already occurring represent the best of the human spirit and the essence of the pastoral care of the world's religions. We must be willing as a nation to sustain these efforts for however long they are needed.

Humiliation is the handmaiden of betrayal. Humiliation clears the way for betrayal. These acts of the terrorists betrayed the universal conventions of human decency and justice in a civilized world. While human aggression may be an intrinsic part of human nature, societies have created controls on human destruction, primarily through rules of law, concepts of fairness and neighborliness, and the Golden Rule. These values are now threatened. This is the ultimate evil of betrayal and humiliation.

America must seek justice for these crimes against humanity. This is part of the healing process. We must also avoid at all costs being tricked by human betrayal into acting without preserving our sense of justice and fairness. We all cringe at terrorists who might have lived in America and shared the goodness of our society with their family members while planning this atrocity. Our rage is cosmic and even at times homicidal because of our feeling of humiliation, especially as all Americans feel violated, used, and unappreciated.

The terrorists and mass murderers of our modern world prey on the humiliation of the average citizens of their own societies for personal aggrandizement. This is another form of betrayal. As we strike out justly against these international criminals, America must not further humiliate their victims within their own societies. America must act wisely and in solidarity with victims of mass violence throughout the world.

Mass violence teaches us lessons at all levels of human existence. All of us, as human beings around the world, are fragile and in need of affection and support throughout our lives. Humiliation and betrayal are forms of evil aimed at destroying these fragile threads of human life, and our sense of being connected to one another.

Some of us will remain the same, and some of us will be different as a result of last Tuesday's events. All of us can become better through our efforts to unite as a nation to respond to a common enemy, but also to unite ourselves as people by crossing boundaries of the various "isms" that have historically divided us. This is a part of my patriot's dream for America.

We improve our common life when we recognize that our society and world are diverse across cultures and within ethnic groups. Our natural resources are scarce, and their exploitation primarily for profit is a sin. Our ability and willingness to change our attitudes and behaviors that do not foster life, and our willingness to adapt to changes we cannot control improves our quality of life. To be inclusive requires hard work and affects our attitudes and how we see other people, the world, and ourselves.

I hope our response as a nation to those who caused the misery that we feel will not be more violence. I pray that we find a nonviolent way, and receive the help of our global neighbors who also feel the threat of what we have experienced, to bring those responsible before a court of law. You arrest individuals, not a nation.

We can find the courage and faith in God to take the risks involved in building a stronger America and find healing through how we relate to one another. Evidence of our capacity to do this is around us and is particularly seen in the endless ways people are responding and helping at the various places were the destruction of human life occurred on Tuesday.

Here in this university community, Yale has been and will continue to demonstrate its best in response to this tragedy. Faculty members, students, and staff members each in their own way are giving of themselves to help those in need and to further our understanding of the complex issues we now face, and some of their ethical and moral challenges and implications.

This may indeed be this college generation's time to respond in ways that will have a positive impact on the quality of life in America and around the world. Your generation is being called by this challenge to seek ways for making global peace and to address the issues of poverty, racism, sexism, and religious bigotry here at home and throughout the world.

My belief in the promise of America has not been destroyed by what happened on September 11. We, as a nation of people, can meet the challenge of rising above many of our differences and lift the burden of our current pain.

My Christian patriot's dream for America allows me to painfully accept and go beyond the tears of the humiliation and mass violence of last Tuesday. I find comfort, strength, direction, and hope in the very words that are also most challenging to hear at this time (Matthew 5:3-9):

Blessed are the poor in spirit, for theirs is the kingdom of heaven.
Blessed are those who mourn, for they will be comforted.
Blessed are the meek, for they will inherit the earth.
Blessed are those who hunger and thirst for righteousness, for they will be filled.
Blessed are the merciful, for they will receive mercy.
Blessed are the pure in heart, for they will see God.
Blessed are the peacemakers, for they will be called children of God.

These attitudes are a blessing to those who seek to appropriate them as a way of life, and it is through them that we are helped to imagine and bring into reality a new community worthy of the name America. I will lift my voice once again today and sing my prayer for America:

O beautiful for spacious skies, for amber waves of grain;
For purple mountain majesties above the fruited plain!
America! America! God shed his grace on thee,
And crown thy good with brotherhood from sea to shining sea.

O beautiful for patriot dream that sees beyond the years;
Thine alabaster cities gleam, undimmed by human tears!
America! America! God shed his grace on thee,
And crown thy good with brotherhood from sea to shining sea.

America! America! America!

Twenty-five

A Day of Terror: Is There a Balm in Gilead?

Helen Lee Turner
Daniel Chapel, Furman University

(Psalm 113; Jeremiah 8:18–9:1; 1 Timothy 2:1-7)

"O that my head were a spring of water, and my eyes a fountain of tears, so that I might weep day and night for the slain of my poor people! . . . Is there no balm in Gilead?" says Jeremiah (9:1; 8:22).

It is as if the prophet knew what we are feeling. Like the people of Judah, who in that day were known the world around for their healing ointment, so we are a people who have believed we possess the cure for all the world's ills.

But now we need the cure, and we are not at all sure where to find it. Our hearts and souls are in need of a healing balm. The writer of 1 Timothy also speaks profoundly across the centuries to contemporary Americans. If ever we need to pray for our leaders and all those in authority the world around, today is the day.

Sometimes the biblical readings from the common lectionary do have almost a miraculous way of speaking to our need. The passages read here today are also being read in churches all across our country, both Catholic and Protestant. They are taken from a schedule of readings called the common lectionary, established by an interdenominational body as appropriate texts to guide us through the church year. If we are in worship every Sunday for three years in churches that use the lectionary, we will hear all of the most significant texts in the entire Bible.

Preaching from the lectionary not only encourages use of seasonally appropriate readings but also pushes ministers to let the Bible speak in sermons. Clergy who use the lectionary cannot simply go and find a biblical text to attach to their own ideas. Instead, they must first listen to the Bible. That, I think, is a good thing. Today Jeremiah's lament and 1 Timothy's instruction speak to me, and I imagine they speak to you without my forcing them to.

But occasionally, lectionary and current events can come together in ways that seem almost too miraculous. If we had read today the assigned Gospel text from Luke, we would have heard about the conniving steward who, about to be dismissed from his job, went around dishonestly lowering the figures on the promissory notes held by those who owed his boss money.

When I lose my job, he thought, *these grateful debtors will take me in.* His plot worked even better than expected. In the end, the master commended the devious manager because he had acted shrewdly, unlike the so-called "children of light." Isn't that what the United States government is doing? We are going around the world shrewdly making promises to those whom we usually regard as our enemies so that we might accomplish what we believe is a greater good? Aren't we following the Gospel for this day?

And if we have any doubt, the psalm that was supposed to be read with the Jeremiah passage (not the one we read, but the one that was supposed to be read) confirms what many of us feel. Hear selections from Psalm 79:

O God, the nations have come into your inheritance; . . .
They have given the bodies of your servants

> to the birds of the air for food. . . .
> They have poured out [your servants'] blood like water. . . .
> We have become a taunt to our neighbors,
>   mocked and derided. (vv. 1-4)

Yes! The Bible is telling us it is time for us to scheme and even to make what may be dishonest deals so that we can strike back against the forces of terror that are mocking us. I am not so sure. Indeed, I do not believe that the Bible was given to us as a divining rod for political action or as a crystal ball for the future. Sometimes what seems obvious is not the whole truth after all. And that is why I chose to use the alternate psalm, number 113, instead of Psalm 79 as our text. The latter seemed just a little too providential.

Healing and salvation surely are more mysterious than that. For me, connecting Psalm 79 with our present sorrow, fear, and anger, makes it too easy to simplistically agree with the statement made by Bob Jones III in Friday's *Greenville Journal*: "These are wicked, evil people bent on the destruction of America. We should show them no mercy. They have shown the world no mercy." Certainly the hijackers were wicked and merciless, and we must clearly identify evil as evil; but neither our healing nor our salvation will come from more death, and especially not from a retribution that gives little thought to the collateral terror that will undoubtedly be a by-product. Where is the infinite justice in that?

Sometimes what seems to be a serendipitous coupling of text and context is really a land mine waiting to explode. I think that is the case today with the lectionary readings, but might it also be the case with the text, the spin we give to the news events themselves? Perhaps we are making connections and drawing conclusions far too quickly. Scheming with the powers of this world may be what our diplomats need to do, but the faithful are called upon in the meantime to look more closely at the rest of the story.

September 11. It was a day of terror, unspeakable, unimagined terror. Even those of us who were far away and knew no one in the towering inferno, need a balm, a cure for the terrors of this nightmare. God help those who lived through it and will live through it for the rest of their lives.

But perhaps, despite the utter horror we have witnessed, we are too preoccupied by our national tragedy to see the other terrors that loom around us, other terrors that may even speak to the larger situation. Bob Jones in that same statement in the *Greenville Journal* is right about one thing: there are other terrors in our world, terrors which are the product of sin. But as troubling as the sins on his list are to some people, I am quite certain he has not correctly identified the truly horrifying abominations of our day, for they are the terrors we seldom notice.

We are a culture that has lost its ability to feel healthy guilt or pity. Daniel Maguire, an ethicist at Marquette University, has said, "The absence of pity is the root of all evil." And at times we seem to have pity on no one but ourselves. We don't want to hear about the pain and burdens of the world. We are quite certain that those things are neither our fault nor our problem. But our attackers pinpointed the reasons for their outrage. They struck at what they saw as "the twin towers of our indifference to the plight of so many and at our haughty military heart," says Maguire.

And though most of them would never wish to kill us, the poor of the world see an absence of pity in our economic policies. For example, 1.3 billion people of the world are in absolute poverty. Eighty-three percent of the world's wealth goes to 20 percent of the people, and most of the wealthy are Americans. While we lie in the lap of luxury, forty million people die yearly from hunger and hunger-related causes. This is like three hundred twenty jumbo jets crashing every day, with half the passengers children. That is a terror that we have far too long ignored.

Perhaps we should have heard the alternate Old Testament reading as well as the alternate psalm, but I was too much of a coward to use it as a text. Amos 8:4-6 includes the following words, "Hear this, you that trample on the needy, and bring to ruin the poor of the land. . . . We . . . practice deceit . . . buying the poor for silver and the needy for a pair of sandals."

That is the word of Amos for today. Surely we think, we hope, the text is not talking about us, the people in this place; but should we at least stop long enough to ask ourselves how we might be complicit by our lack of real pity? Is the attack on America by zealous hijackers the only terror calling out for justice? Maybe the lectionary does contain the word of God for today after all.

Anyone who has endured my Introduction to Religion class has heard about the four biblical passages Old Testament scholar Phyllis Trible calls the texts of terror. These are texts, or parts of texts, we usually ignore. They aren't the main story, or so we think. They are the stories of Hagar, a slave woman used, abused, and rejected; Tamar, the princess raped and discarded; an unnamed concubine mentioned in the book of Judges who was raped, murdered, and dismembered; and the daughter of Jephthah, the virgin who becomes the sacrificial victim of her father's foolish bargain. These are stories of women who endure terrifying ordeals and die unremembered, women whose suffering goes without judgment or justice even in the biblical text. Many of you have never even heard these stories, but I assure you they are there. The fate of these women is either forgotten, not only by us but by the text itself. Their pain is overshadowed by the stories of the superpowers of the biblical tradition— Abraham, David, the Levite, the mighty warrior. Or even worse, the plight of these women is discounted completely in our interpretation of their lives. Hagar's slavery is part of God's greater plan, some say. Jephthah had to keep his promise to God, say others, thus justifying the human sacrifice of the general's daughter. The concubine was, after all, an immoral prostitute; and using her kept the men from committing the sin of homosexuality. A greater plan was at work, don't you see?

But Phyllis Trible does not see. These deaths, these rapes, are terrifying sacrifices and must be remembered, says Trible. So, for each woman Trible erects an imaginary tombstone with epitaphs that echo the epitaphs we associate with Jesus. Epitaphs we read during Holy Week when we think of our Lord's painful death on the cross. Trible's gravestones read thusly. "Hagar, Egyptian slave woman. She was wounded for our transgressions; she was bruised for our iniquities. Tamar, princess of Judah, a woman of sorrows and acquainted with grief. An unnamed woman, concubine from Bethlehem, her body was broken and given to many. The daughter of Jephthah, virgin of Gilead; my God, my God why hast thou forsaken her?"[1]

Are these epitaphs blasphemy? Some would say so. But I ask, Are they a vital ingredient in the saving balm? Perhaps the answer is partly in what has happened to us as a people as we recount the sacrifices of hundreds of firefighters and police, as we praise the heroic acts of ordinary people in an airplane that crashed in a field in Pennsylvania, or as we shed tears at the report of an orthodox Jew who refused to abandon his quadriplegic Christian friend on the 27th floor of a tower that killed them both.

We are changed. For now at least we are more loving, more caring, more in touch with those around us and their needs. I dare say we are more alive. Even great financial entities like the television networks have stopped their quest for economic gain long enough to cooperate with each other and to give to someone else. We have found a new sense of purpose as we unite to remember these sacrificial victims, all of them in some sense making the meaning of the death of Christ real for us. They are the suffering Christ in our world.

But the balm will lose its power if we move now to seek

181

revenge rather than a justice informed by love and mercy. The balm will become dry and useless if we see more death as the only answer. What we have felt in the last few days as the beginning of healing will become a temporary remission if we do not recognize that our heroes are not the only ones with whom Christ died. They are not the only ones who can offer us this remedy, this grace. We must see, we must remember, the other innocent victims, the victims of poverty, of disease, of abuse, the victims of our own wealth.

They too will heal us. For, you see, the death of Christ, while it was for us the beginning of our salvation, was not a unilateral act that touches us only as a past event. The power that gives and sustains life, the power that frees us from sin, does not flow directly from the crucified and resurrected savior to us in the form of dogma, a necessary belief. If indeed believing that Jesus died for our sin is the only necessary thing, there is no salvation, no healing balm in it. Instead the cross becomes an excuse, a justification for our indifference to the pain of this world.

It even becomes a means to perpetuate suffering and death. If we wait for the past event of the death of Christ alone to heal us, no almighty power will deliver us from evil. Belief in this one heroic, divine deed will not conquer oppressive powers and death-delivering systems.[2] Faith in the transforming power of Christ's death, faith that is experienced, lived, acted on, not just believed, is the answer. There is the true infinite justice.

Christ did not die for us once, but thousands and millions of times in the lives of all the world's victims. The community of the faithful sustains the life-giving power of the cross by remembering and believing in that one event. The life-giving power of the cross is made real among the community of the faithful by the memory of its own brokenheartedness and by the memory and awareness of all those who have suffered and continue to suffer, not only those who are victims of terrorist hijackers but also those who are victims of an economic system that allows them to die without pity. The death of Jesus and the death of the American terrorist victims are not a call to despair or even a call to cling to the cross of Jesus for hope. Instead, these deaths are a call to actualize the saving power of the cross; they are a call to us to do our part to end suffering. It is our call to do what Psalm 113 says God does.

It is our call to bring life out of barrenness. This is our call to experience and live the faith brought to us first through the cross of Christ.

Is there a balm in Gilead? In America? Yes! It is to be found on the crosses of all victims of this world with whom Christ dies.

Notes

1 Phyllis Trible, *Texts of Terror: Literary-Feminist Readings of Biblical Narratives* (Philadelphia: Fortress, 1984).

2. Some of the ideas and phrasing in this paragraph and the next are from Rita Nakashima Brock's book *Journeys by Heart: A Christology of Erotic Power* (New York: Crossroad, 1988).

Twenty-six

In the Darkness, Light

William H. Willimon
Duke University Chapel

(Genesis 1:1-11; John 1:1-5)

I had another sermon prepared to preach in New Haven. My title, "Why God Is Bigger than Yale," was rendered instantly inappropriate. On Tuesday, I tossed it and started driving home from the Midwest. Like you, I will not forget where I was when the earth heaved, and the sky turned dark, and death reigned.

In a motel room in South Dakota, for just one moment I turned away from the trivialities of morning TV. And when I looked again, the image—the ball of fire, plume of smoke—a world deconstructed. A building, a tower touching the heavens, is rubble, and mothers weep, and a man runs down the street screaming, "I want to kill somebody!"

Robert J. Lifton, in a radio interview last week, spoke of a "profound sense of vulnerability" particularly among a people who think of ourselves as a "superpower." Though our leaders reassured us of security, retaliation, vengeance, and normalcy, and sent ships to sea to prove it, that wasn't what most of us got. What we got was vulnerability ("I had just kissed her good-bye at the airport," he said), fragility ("If this can happen, I mean, my God what else?" said another). Out of control.

We have now had five hard days of numbed, grieved silence. What now can be said? What were the first words God said? God said, "Let there be light" (this, by the way, was the first text I preached on my first Sunday in Duke Chapel seventeen years ago):

> When God [began creating] the heavens and the earth, the earth was a formless void . . . darkness covered the face of the deep, . . . a wind from God swept over the face of the waters. Then God said, "Let there be light"; and there was light. And God saw that the light was good. (Genesis 1:1-4)

We believe these verses originated during Israel's exile, amid hopelessness and despair engendered by having your country pillaged, your temple ruined, your cities wrecked. In other words, this sermon, Genesis 1, was first preached amid national desolation. Thrashing about for a text for you, I thought of Genesis 1.

In the beginning all was night, a "formless void." In the Hebrew, "formless void," is *tohu wa bohu*. *Tohu wa bohu*. Even if you don't know Hebrew, you know it's bad. *Tohu wa bohu* more truthfully tells what happened to our collective consciousness this Tuesday past than "America under attack" or "civilization in peril."

How well the Bible names us. God's first creative word was addressed not to any of us, but to that formless, bubbling chaos.

God just said, "Light!" And there was, just by the command of God. Then, "Land! Trees! Humanity!" and it was "good, very good." But first God, then light. Whenever there is creation out of chaos, light in the gloom, or something out of the primal *tohu wa bohu,* that's good, that's God.

What God spoke into being on that first day keeps happening. Note I didn't render it, "When God once upon a time created the heavens and the earth," but rather "When God began creating the heavens and the earth." Creation, according to the opening verb, is not finished, complete, done. Creation is a work in progress. If God should withdraw his powerful hand from the world, for even a moment, all would be lost, said Calvin. Every day we are dependent on God to keep doing what God did in Genesis 1.

God takes the threatening *tohu wa bohu* and fashions it into what we name as beauty, order, creation, peace. What God did, God does. Creation is in the future tense.

This week we have all been to school. We have learned our lesson: this world, at one moment so stable, secure, fixed, and reliable, is more fragile that it seems. The CIA was clueless, airport security an oxymoron, and innocent people, just trying to do their job, horribly hurt. I looked into the faces of the perpetrators, desperate for a glimpse of how, why their humanity could have been so defaced to lead them to such violence. I wished there had been only one of them to explain away.

That afternoon, when a door slammed at the rental car agency where I begged for a car, I almost ducked and covered. Call me crazy but, in my defense, Lifton is right: people who've had a world pulled out from under them are pushed to irrationality and fear.

Yet maybe our feelings of vulnerability and fragility are the closest we've come to rationality in a long time. Maybe we are really more exposed than we thought. Maybe it was madness to assume that we are in charge; that the war with Iraq ended threat of war; that in arming the Afghan rebels against Soviets they would never turn their guns toward us; that decades of injustice and poverty, of escalating violence could be kept over there and never here. Maybe Jesus was right in his dire predictions of what happens to those who take up the sword.

I'm sure that in ancient Israel there were folk who sincerely believed that the thick walls around Jerusalem couldn't be breached, that the vast Temple would stand forever. And when this crumbled in a weekend, dark despair went with them into exile. It was night. It was like that cloud covering the sun on a once-perfect Manhattan September day.

And what then? In the most bleak days of their exile, isn't it amazing that Israel risked some of its most pushy, strong poetry like Genesis 1? Declaring in full-throated joy, "In the beginning, when there was nothing but *tohu wa bohu*, then God said, 'Let there be light!' And there was."

I would have thought the first word might be *vengeance*, or *cowering fear*, or at least *bitterness*. But no, the first word the exiles heard God say to *tohu wa bohu* was, "Light!" And there was, and it was good.

It is a word that we cannot say to ourselves. It must be spoken to us, overheard in God's conversation with the formless void. No word—not mine, or the president's, or some grief counselor, or therapist—can help us when the chips are down, and the mountains tremble, and the earth shakes; no word can help except one spoken from the outside. And just at full midnight we hear that word, and it is a sovereign command, a promise, a creative act: "Light!"

I was wrong to look into the faces of terrorists, hoping to find some consoling answer. There is nothing in the hands of Congress that can heal the wound that we have suffered. The trouble between us and the resilient *tohu wa bohu* is serious. If there is not a God who delights in bringing light out of night, who likes nothing better than to go one-on-one with *tohu wa bohu*, then we are quite frankly without hope, and my little words of comfort in the face of your despair are pointless.

The good news: God's will for the world will not be stumped. You were right to look for clues in the faces of heroic firefighters and heroic mothers who, even having had the one most dear to them ripped from them in death, are heroically not bitter, not hate-filled. The creative lover that had the first word shall also have the last. All evidence to the

187

contrary, God's love is stronger than human hate because that's the way God has set up the world.

In life and death, in life beyond death, there is only one word. At the end, it's the same word as at the beginning, that by God the light shines in the darkness, and the darkness has not overcome it (John 1:5).

Twenty-seven

Homily at Methesco Seminary

Bill Wylie-Kellermann
Methodist Theological School

> How lonely sits the city that once was full of people!
> How like a widow she has become,
>   she that was great among the nations! . . .
> She weeps bitterly in the night,
>   with tears on her cheeks;
> among all her lovers
>   she has no one to comfort her; . . .
> The roads to Zion mourn,
>   for no one comes to the festivals;
> all her gates are desolate. (Lamentations 1:1-4)

> By the rivers of Babylon—
>   there we sat down and there we wept
>   when we remembered Zion. (Psalm 137:1)

By rights, standing before you as a representative of SCUPE (Seminary Consortium for Urban Pastoral Education), I ought to handpick a text invoking the vitality of the city and provoking calls to ministry—or at least to taste and test such calls. Instead the lectionary, which so often astonishes in its providence, has set before us a stunning text of urban desolation and tears at a moment exactly thus.

I know that in the days since September 11, tears of grief have been freely shed in this place, and for that I give thanks. They are part of the church's work, both pastoral and prophetic, which Walter Brueggemann calls "the public embrace of pain."

Those tears are not only or even largely for ourselves, but for others. They are tears of intercession. As Bonhoeffer writes in *Life Together*, to intercede is to feel another's pain or need so deeply that we pray their prayer. From their place. In their stead. For their sake. They are tears that open for us the work of spiritual solidarity.

This attack connects us, as never before in the U.S., with others who have suffered. We are suddenly linked with those beneath bombs and subject to violence. The question is put: Can we look on the rubble of Manhattan and see Baghdad or Beirut or Ramallah?

It is an urgent pastoral (and perhaps as well political) insight to understand that suffering, especially innocent suffering, can be justifying. I use this word precisely in Saint Paul's sense of constructing a self-righteous idolatry. I think, for example, of the Holocaust, a truly innocent suffering on a vastly different scale, but theologically edifying. So many of those who passed through that horror witnessed to a renewed vision of humanity, a moral passion on behalf of all those who anywhere suffer violence and injustice. But that same history, those same events, the same anguish of suffering, can also be invoked to sanction exclusion, demolition, assassination, air strikes, and Palestinian apartheid. The meaning of suffering and death is partly a moral choice, theologically put.

When I was ordained a deacon, under the older process, I placed my hand on a Bible open to Psalm 137 and was asked to receive authority to preach the Word and administer the

190

sacraments. That psalm, which also forms part of the lectionary readings this week, is indeed one close to my heart and ministry. And yet we rarely read it to the end, sparing ourselves the embarrassing scandal of its punchline: happy is the one who shall seize your children and dash them against the rocks (v. 9). This psalm, among others, articulates how grief may turn to rage. It is prayerfully honest, utterly so, about this connection. And we should be alert to it as well in the present moment.

Those who I find most thoughtful about recent events have begun to ask, What is the suffering behind the rage of which we are now recipients? This is a question no longer pastorally premature to a people in grief. In chapter 1 of Lamentations, suffering leads to self-examination in history and before God. It is timely for us to ask, What is the injustice of the global economy for which the World Trade Center towers have become an emblem to the world? What are the oil-based and cold war incursions, open and clandestine, that the U.S. has made over so long a time in the Middle East? And speaking of clandestine, can we acknowledge what does not appear in the easy histories portrayed in our national media, that the largest covert operation ever mounted by the U.S. effectively supported Bin Laden's terrorism against the Soviet Union, contributing to its collapse? Can we recognize our hand in the very operation that enabled the Taliban to take power? These are hard questions for us. And very hard to put in the present moment.

I can't help but think today of Jesus' tears for the city. I think of the form that his own lamentation over Jerusalem takes. I believe he foresaw the destruction of the city and grieved in love. Since the Gospels were largely written after the destruction of the Second Temple, it is widely suggested that the Gospel writers have filled in the details of his vision. Nonetheless, I'm convinced he foresaw it not so much in some omniscient sense, but in the manner of reading the signs of the times. He could see coming the violent uprising against the Roman occupation and against the injustice of Temple complicity in it. And once that, it didn't take much to imagine the Roman boot coming down.

In that sense, the kingdom movement and, finally, the cross signify a concrete historical alternative, the way to break a terrible cycle of violence. In the forgiving love of the cross, even the love of enemies, Christ broke that cycle. He broke the rule of death and so disarmed the powers.

Because of his, our tears are made the very form of faith. They finally issue not in rage of vengeance, but in love—and so in hope for the city. Amen.

Afterword

The Sunday After Tuesday: An Afterword

Stanley Hauerwas
Duke University

September 11, 2001, is not the day that changed our world. The world, the cosmos, what we call history, was changed in A.D. 33. Preaching after September 11, 2001, requires that what happened on September 11, 2001, be narrated in the light of cross and resurrection. To be sure, this is a task easier said than done. I do not relish the task these preachers faced. Stilled and stunned, stunned to silence, it was their duty to preach, to proclaim the good news of the gospel. It is not for me, one who does not have the responsibility to preach the word of God, to praise or criticize, to stand in judgment, on these sermons.

I cannot even say I am glad I have had to read these sermons. In the face of September 11, I distrust words. I fear, no matter how hard we try to say what needs to be said, what we say may threaten to explain when no explanation is possible. For me, a person seldom at a loss for words, I find my continuing reaction to September 11, 2001, to be one of silence. I simply do not know what to say. At least one of the reasons I have nothing to say is because I am a pacifist. I am, whether

I like it or not, committed to Christian nonviolence. The horror, the terror, the strange beauty of the violence on September 11, calls for a response, a violent response. Being a pacifist does nothing to free me from the desire to set things right by punishing those who perpetrated such an outrage. Conflicted, I remain silent, fearing any words I may say would suggest a confidence I do not have.

Yet surely it is a good thing the church required those ordained to preach the gospel to stand before their congregations the Sunday after September 11, 2001. That they were able to do so draws on the hope made possible by cross and resurrection. Of course what they said is important, but at least as important is that they had no choice but to proclaim that God is God and we are not. The difficult challenge, however, is to proclaim the gospel without the proclamation being captured by false comforts.

For example, I do not envy the challenge these preachers faced, determined as it was by to whom they were preaching. Were they preaching to Americans or Christians? The claim that September 11, 2001, forever changed the world is a claim shaped by the narrative of being an American. As Americans, we feel violated, vulnerable, fearful. We hate those who have made us recognize our fear. We hate those who have made it impossible for us to trust our neighbors. We hate the loss of security, the loss of comfort that comes from routine. We want normality. I think we are right to want all this, but we must remember that these desires—if we are Christians—must be shaped by our fear of God.

I often try to explain the work I have done in theology and ethics by telling the joke about the Lone Ranger and Tonto. It seems that the Lone Ranger and Tonto found themselves surrounded by twenty thousand Sioux in South Dakota. The Lone Ranger turned to Tonto and said, "This looks like a pretty tough situation, Tonto. What do you think we ought to do?" Tonto responded, "What do you mean by 'we,' white man?" I use this joke to suggest why my work has been an attempt to help Christians reclaim the Christian "we." For example, when George Bush declared at the beginning of the Gulf War that we must oppose "naked aggression" wherever it occurs, unfortunately too many Christians assumed they were included in that "we."

My use of this joke, however, risks not only being out of date (few college students even know who the Lone Ranger was), but also may oversimplify. The joke seems to suggest that we must choose between being Christian or American. But our lives are too entangled with the stories that make us American and Christian for easy separation. The sermons in this book rightly reflect and struggle with the inseparability of those stories. Inseparable though the stories may be, however, it is crucial, if we are to preach the gospel, that the stories that constitute America not be allowed to determine what we as Christians must say and hear.

In his introduction, William Willimon observes that churches that lacked substantive liturgical habits had fewer resources to resist the American flag becoming the central symbol for congregational worship. I am sure Willimon is right to suggest that if our sanctuaries are empty they will be filled with alien forms of life. Of course red, white, and blue are Christian colors. Red is Pentecost, white is Easter, and blue is Mary's color; but for Christians these colors are never sewn together. Unfortunately, when they are sewn together, they threaten to overwhelm, if not replace, their role in reflecting as well as forming our vision as God's people.

Willimon also suggests that, in the absence of determinative liturgical forms, it is not surprising that some of the sermons after September 11, 2001, offer humanistic advice aimed at taking away or at least assuaging the pain. Indeed, some of these sermons seem to try to "get God off the hook" or, failing that, to show that even though we cannot understand how God could allow this to happen to people like us, believing in God remains important if we are not to be crushed by the terror of September 11, 2001. As under-

195

standable, as human as these responses are, I think they fail
to be appropriately disciplined by the gospel. Christians—at
least Christians who Sunday after Sunday read the psalms—
should know the question "Why do bad things happen to
good people?" is not a question Christians should ask.

Which is but a reminder that more important than sermons preached after September 11, 2001, is the kind of
preaching that shaped the life of congregations prior to
September 11, 2001. For if Christians had no way of discern-
ing how their being Christian might involve tension with
being American prior to September 11, you can be sure that
they, or those who preached to them after that date, would
be unable to say how the Christian response can and must be
distinguished from the American response. The sentimen-
tality and pietism that is so prominent in American sermon-
izing could not help but grip our imaginations and speech
when confronted by the horrible events of this day.

For example, I have tried to think how Augustine might
have responded to September 11, 2001. After all he wrote
The City of God at least in part to make clear that it was not
Christianity that made Rome vulnerable to the barbarians.
According to Augustine, Rome was only reaping what
Roman pride had sown. Augustine asks us to consider the
somewhat surprising fact that something in humility exalts
the mind, and something in exaltation abases the mind.

> But devout humility makes the mind subject to what is supe-
> rior. Nothing is superior to God; and that is why humility
> exalts the mind by making it subject to God. Exaltation, in
> contrast, derives from a fault in character, and spurns sub-
> jection for that very reason. Hence it falls away from him who
> has no superior, and falls lower in consequence. . . . That is
> why humility is highly prized in the City of God and especial-
> ly enjoined on the City of God during the time of its pil-
> grimage in this world; and it receives particular emphasis in
> the character of Christ, the king of that City. We are also
> taught by the sacred Scriptures that the fault of exaltation,

the contrary of humility, exercises supreme dominion in Christ's adversary, the Devil. This is assuredly the great difference that sunders the two cities of which we are speaking: the one is a community of devout men, the other a company of the irreligious, and each has its own angels attached to it. In one city love of God has been given first place, in the other, love of self. (*The City of God*, 14, 13) [1]

Ask yourself when was the last time you preached or heard a sermon that suggested that most of our lives are determined by pride? When was the last time you preached or heard a sermon that named how we are possessed because of our pride by the powers that take the form of institutions we assume we "control"? When was the last time you heard or preached a sermon that intimated that the pride in "Proud to Be an American" might not be a "good thing," given what Christians think about pride? Jerry Falwell was, of course, wrong to suggest that what happened was a judgment on American divorce and abortion cultures. He was not only wrong, but the god he assumed was doing the judgment is not the Christian God. After all, God does not punish us for our sins, but our sins are punishment. Yet I cannot help but think that Augustine might well have seen in those proud buildings, those elegant buildings, manifestation of a pride that knows not the humility of Christ.

Let me be clear. I am not suggesting that the people that died on September 11, 2001, "deserved" their deaths. Nor am I suggesting that we should see in that horrible destruction the direct hand of God. Rather, I am simply pointing out that, as Christians, we have been lazy in our speech habits and, in particular, in our sermons just to the extent we have failed to help one another name how our lives are caught in modes of life Augustine identified with the City of Man. We have allowed God to be relegated to the realm of the "personal," and as a result we have no way to narrate America in the way Augustine narrated Rome.

Some of the sermons in this collection at least suggested that we could not afford to think of what happened on September 11, 2001, without remembering the abuses to the world perpetrated in the name of America as well as the lives lost daily through starvation and poverty. Those who called our attention to these abuses (if that is not too easy a word) did so without in any way excusing or justifying the murders perpetrated on September 11, 2001. I think it is right and good to remind us that what happened on September 11, 2001, did not cancel the many wrongs that have been and continue to be done in the name of America. Yet we must be careful not to let what happened on September 11 become an occasion for us to trot out our views, views well formed before September 11, about what is wrong with America.

I think there is much wrong with America. I think there is and continues to be much wrong with American foreign policy. Yet I must be careful, as those who have the courage to hold up those wrongs in sermons, to theologically discipline my outrage. For example, the sense of unity Americans seem to feel after September 11, 2001, is surely a judgment on the church. Unity is what we are about as Christians. Eucharist is the feast of unity. That Christians find themselves captured by the unity offered by the flag is surely a sign that the church has been less than God called us to be. That unity is the same unity that makes us so hesitant to kill in the name of loyalties less than our loyalty to Christ.

Which finally brings me back to silence. Silence inhabits the edges of our words. If we are to preach truthfully after September 11, 2001, we must not try to say too much. We must not pretend we have an answer to explain what happened or know what response we—and who is the "we"?—might make. I have no pacifist foreign policy. I believe the church is God's foreign policy. Which makes it all the more important that we be able truthfully to preach God's Word. I wished I had a sermon I might share as one attempt to preach God's Word after September 11, 2001. I have nothing so developed as a sermon, but I do have a prayer. It was a prayer I wrote as a devotion to begin a Duke Divinity School Council meeting. I was able to write the prayer because of a short article I had just read in the *Houston Catholic Worker* by Jean Vanier (November 16, 2001).[2] My only prayer is that my prayer is to the God who, in the face of terror, miraculously calls forth lives like Jean Vanier, who believes God has saved us from violence by giving us the good work of living with those called "retarded."

Great God of surprise, our lives continue to be haunted by the specter of September 11, 2001. Life must go on, and we go on keeping on—even meeting again as the Divinity School Council. Is this what Barth meant in 1933 when he said we must go on "as though nothing had happened"? To go on as though nothing has happened can sound like a counsel of despair, of helplessness, of hopelessness. We want to act, to do something to reclaim the way things were. Which, I guess, is but a reminder that one of the reasons we are so shocked, so violated, by September 11 is the challenge presented to our prideful presumption that we are in control, that we are going to get out of life alive. To go on "as though nothing had happened" surely requires us to acknowledge you are God and we are not. It is hard to remember that Jesus did not come to make us safe, but rather he came to make us disciples, citizens of your new age, a kingdom of surprise. That we live in the end times is surely the basis for our conviction that you have given us all the time we need to respond to September 11 with "small acts of beauty and tenderness," which, Jean Vanier tells us, if done with humility and confidence, "will bring unity to the world and break the chain of violence." So we pray, give us humility that we may remember the work we do today, the work we do every day, is false and pretentious if it fails to serve those who day in and day out are your small gestures of beauty and tenderness.

199

Notes

1. Augustine, *The City of God,* David Knowles, trans. (New York: Penguin Books, 1972), 14, 13, pp. 572-73.

2. Jean Vanier, "L'Arch Founder Responds to Violence," *Houston Catholic Worker,* November 16, 2001, p. 7.

Discussion Guide

William H. Willimon writes, "A great trauma makes theologians of us all." This book challenges us to think about God and our faith in the face of a terrible tragedy. If you are discussing this book with others, this guide offers four sessions for group use. It will take from forty-five minutes to a hour for each meeting. Plan for the final ten minutes to be spent in individual introspection on the personal reflection question. Paper and pencils will be needed. A short final prayer to conclude the session is printed at the end of each lesson.

Session One: So Many Questions

1. Many questions were raised in this volume. Read through the following list gleaned from the sermons. Mark the top two questions that you struggled with after September 11. If your key question is not listed, please add it on the blank line provided.

Why did this happen to us?
Where are you, God?

Is there really a God?
Why did God allow such evil to destroy such innocence?
Is a disaster like this God's will?
What causes someone to act so that another will die?
What is left when everything we have is taken from us?
What does this mean?
What is Jesus doing now?
When we are threatened or afraid, who (or what) is our refuge?
What is going to happen next?
Who will deliver us from evil?

---

2. Were there any questions that you could not ask or that were silenced by the mass impact of the tragedy? William H. Willimon writes, "When the Empire is in jeopardy, solidarity is required, not potentially divisive critical questioning, must less sober reflection and honesty." Has time forced you to ask new or different questions? Darryl Barrow writes, "[B]eyond the tragic event, an event that defies humanity's explanations, there is a purpose which faith alone can see amid the shadows and which patience will in time reveal." From the vantage point of the present, can you look back and see any purpose in the events of September 11?

3. What is a preacher's role in a time of crisis? Willimon says the great challenge of the Sunday after Tuesday was to lay "the story of the life, death, and resurrection of Jesus over the story of September 11." What do you want from a preacher when you are faced with tragedy or time of great trouble?

4. Willimon says that these sermons taken together "provide a picture of one generation attempting to help

another make sense of a world that has shifted on its axis." What have you heard the elders, the "children of the 1960s" saying to the "millennials," a generation described as "sheltered, parentally protected, . . . closely attached (by way of cell phones) to their parents, . . . ultra-organized, putting a high premium on . . . safety," and "politically apathetic." Do you identify with either generation? What would you like to say to those older or younger than you are? What can you learn from other age groups? Are there some lessons that just can't be learned from someone else?

5. Tim Dearborn asks if September 11 was "the end of the old world and the beginning of a new one, what kind will it be?" He says that Augustine tells us that there are two kinds of cities, one committed to self-love and the other to God's love. What characteristics would you expect each kind of city to honor? Think back to September 11. What behaviors were valued most? How about this week? Think of the top news stories. What is being valued now? What kind of "city" are you living in?

Personal Reflection Question

6. Peter Gomes writes, "Seeking faith amidst the ruins is the subtext of these days." Think back and remember the rescue workers from Ground Zero at the World Trade Center as they carried rubble out by bucketfuls in the early days. What were they looking for? What did you want them to find? Now think symbolically of the ruins of your own life. Are there any tragedies or personal situations that seem hopeless? What must you seek among the rubble? What remnants of hope or fragments of faith are you looking for?

Closing Prayer

God, who is our refuge and strength, our very present help in trouble, help us to not fear, even though the earth changes, the mountains shake in the heart of the sea, and the waters roar and foam. Help us to trust that you are in the midst of our cities, our towns, and our lives and that you will bring help with each morning. Amen. (Adapted from Psalm 46)

.

Session Two: How Do We React to Evil?

1. Several authors suggest that Christians should respond to attack not with embargoes or bombs but by providing food and medicines to those who suffer, even in countries we consider political enemies. After all, Jesus did say, "Love your enemies, do good to those who hate you, bless those who curse you, pray for those who abuse you" (Luke 6:27-28). What do you imagine would have happened if our country had not used military force and had instead focused on aid, diplomacy, and prayer?

2. Tony Campolo asks, "Are we forgetting what Jesus told us?" How do we as Christians wrestle with Jesus' words: "You have heard of old, 'An eye for eye and a tooth for tooth'; but I give you a new commandment. Do good to those who hurt you." Did you want to do good to the hijackers or those who sponsored them? Do you want to do good to others who may hold views similar to theirs? How do what we want to do or feel like acting matter when determining our actions?

3. Are you a patriot? What does this word mean to you? Would you have answered differently before September 11? Simone Weil defined *patriotism* as "tender affection for one's country, ever seeking that which is its best." Does this match your understanding of patriotism? Why or why not?

4. Todd Lake sums up the "pacifist position" toward war as "the conviction that there are many causes worth dying for, but none worth killing for." He writes that the "just war" position allows a "measured response in order to restore peace, as long as noncombatants are not targeted." Which point of view characterizes your beliefs?

Did the military response in Afghanistan meet the criteria for a just war?

5. Stanley Hauerwas writes, "I believe the church is God's foreign policy." If this is true, how might the church best be involved in areas of conflict and warfare?

Personal Reflection Question
6. Frederick Streets writes, "Mass violence teaches us lessons at all levels of human existence. All of us, as human beings around the world, are fragile and in need of affection and support throughout our lives. Humiliation and betrayal are forms of evil aimed at destroying these fragile threads of human life, and our sense of being connected to one another." What parts did humiliation and betrayal play in the tragedy of September 11? Have you ever felt humiliated or betrayed? What emotions did you feel? How did you act or want to act? What actions and values counteract humiliation and betrayal? Who needs your affirmation and support? What steps can you take to make a difference today?

Closing Prayer
God, help us to find the strength and the wisdom today for "small acts of beauty and tenderness," which "will bring unity to the world and break the chain of violence." Amen. (Adapted from Stanley Hauerwas and Jean Vanier)

Session Three: How Do We Live in Troubled Times?

The questions for sessions 3 and 4 focus on the spiritual resources that offer meaning and strength in all times, especially difficult ones. Small groups of two to four people would be appropriate for each of these questions. As before, leave time at the end of your session for the personal reflection question and a closing prayer.

1. Darrell Brazell writes, "Our life is but a mist. We naively believe that we have tomorrow and next week and next year. . . . In this time of crisis we must face the frailty of this life. . . . [W]e must face the futility of our idols." Brazell identifies wealth and the government as places we place our trust rather than relying on God. Where are you tempted to put your trust? Brazell asks, "When a crisis explodes our concept of reality, what value do our idols hold? What power to save do they contain?"

2. Peter Gomes writes, "Do you know the proper meaning of the word *comfort*? . . . It means to 'fortify,' to 'strengthen,' to 'give courage,' even 'power,' and not merely consolation." He continues, "The God of all comfort is the One who gives inner power and strength to those who would be easily outnumbered, outmaneuvered, outpowered by the conventional forces and the conventional wisdom. . . . Inner strength, I believe, comes from the sure conviction that God has placed us in the world to do the work of life, and not death." How have you been comforted in the past? How might this understanding of the word *comfort* change the way you act toward someone who has experienced a great loss or tragedy?

3. James Howell reminds us that Psalm 102 is one of what Roman Catholics call the "Seven Penitential Psalms,"

that are read and cried out during times of intense grief, fear, or sorrow. Read the psalm aloud slowly. Listen for a phrase or image that you can ponder for a while. After the psalm is read, sit quietly and let that phrase or image work in you. Share your reflection with others, if you feel comfortable doing so.

4. The Heidelberg Catechism, Mark Labberton tells us, was written in the sixteenth century. Recite the question-and-answer on comfort, in the knowledge that you join millions of others over the course of five centuries who have reaffirmed their trust in Jesus in the face of death and temptation. Can you affirm your trust that everything must fit God's purpose for your salvation? Why or why not?

Q: What is your only comfort, in life and death?

A: That I belong—body and soul, in life and in death—not to myself but to my faithful Savior, Jesus Christ, who at the cost of his own blood has fully paid for all my sins and has completely freed me from the dominion of the devil; that he protects me so well that without the will of my Father in heaven not a hair can fall from my head; indeed, that everything must fit his purpose for my salvation. Therefore, by his Holy Spirit, he also assures me of eternal life, and makes me wholeheartedly willing and ready from now on to live for him.

5. Read these words written by Mark Labberton: "There is no evidence in the Bible that God wants us to be happy. That's just not there! Joy? Now that's something God wants us to know. Hope? That's something God cares about deeply. Happiness? Happiness in the sense of carefree delight, no problems, easy, no sense of conscience, no particular sense of worry or burden—that's

not in the Bible." Do you agree with him? Why or why not? How would you define *joy* or *hope* from the Bible's point of view?

Personal Reflection Question

6. Reread Elizabeth McGregor Simmons's story on page 167 where she recounts the day she was sitting in a sixth-grade class on the day President Kennedy was shot. She admits that she failed to challenge her teacher, who gloated at the president's assassination. She then writes, "Today I challenge those of you who may sit in a similar place to where I sat on that long ago November day to do better than I did. Cling to the images that Jesus gave us of a God who embraces all of the sheep, and of a woman who shines her light into every nook of darkness; claim these as the very images in which you . . . were created." How can you stand up for God's children who are marginalized or discounted? How is your own future bound up with those who suffer?

Closing Prayer

O God, as we continue to think about what is our only comfort in life and death, gripped as we are by the tragedies we have witnessed, may we reflect on your work, hearing you as our teacher, listening for your voice and allowing you to speak. Comfort, instruct, and lead us, we pray. In the name of Jesus Christ. Amen. (Adapted from Mark Labberton)

Session Four: Living Differently
Because of What We've Seen

1. Several sermons in this volume ask vocational questions. After seeing tragedy, destruction, and loss of innocent life, they ask: What do you want to do with the rest of your life? Using various approaches, several preachers echo Barbara Carlson's belief that "[t]he commitment to act affirmatively for life can deliver us from evil." Laura Majovski tells the stories of three people who are living examples of living out the call of God to service. How does coming face-to-face with the fragility of life have an impact on your choices of what to do with your time and energies? Do you feel called to service? If so, what first steps might you take toward offering your skills and love to others?

2. Scotty McLennan outlines several steps for healing. He suggests that, first, people must unite in community in troubled times. Second, each person must take determined action in service to others. Third, we must have faith in God's healing power and commit ourselves to fifteen minutes each morning and evening to sit quietly in meditation or prayer to be still with God. Finally, we must, in the words of the psalmist, "be strong, and let your heart take courage, all you who hope in the Lord." Barbara Carlson adds some other suggestions: Be gentle with yourselves when in grief. Be gentle with those whose needs are different from your own. Take time for what sustains you and connects you affirmatively and actively with life. Light a candle. Let this personal prayer be your commitment to act in some way for peace this week. How might these actions begin the healing process? What else has helped you to heal?

3. Earl Palmer tells the story of someone asking theologian Karl Barth if "the guilt of Germany" after WWII

could be placed on the shoulders of a captured SS officer. Barth responded, "No, the guilt of Germany has been placed on quite another man's shoulders," referring to Jesus. Where can we place the guilt of the hijackers from September 11? Where would you prefer to place the blame? How do we think about guilt and blame in light of the gospel?

4. William H. Willimon writes that "no real healing" is possible without "confession, repentance, forgiveness, acceptance of responsibility, honesty, speaking the truth in love, and all the other peculiar virtues that are part of Christian worship." Darrell Brazell continues the emphasis on repentance by writing, "[T]he first step of repentance is to confess our sin: confess our sins as a corporate nation; confess sins as a corporate church; confess our sins as individuals." What actions of the United States demand repentance? What responsibilities are ours, and what are not?

5. Reread the story of the telephone operator who talked to and recited the Lord's Prayer with a passenger on United Flight 93. It is retold by Laura Majovski on page 132. The telephone operator was just doing her job and was called upon to become the last ministering link between a man and his family, an airplane full of people, and the nation that later would be inspired by their heroic actions. What does this story tell you about how God uses unexpected people to care for others in dire distress? What would you hope to do if put in her position? How can you prepare now to be ready to answer another's call for help?

Personal Reflection Question
6. Peter Gomes describes the baptismal tradition of the Greek Orthodox Church in which the priest takes a

very large pectoral cross and strikes the infant forcibly to leave the sign of the cross on the child, symbolically indicating that "the child who has been baptized into Christ must bear the cross, and that the cross is a sign not of ease or of victory or of prosperity or of success, but of sorrow, suffering, pain, and death; and by it those things are overcome." By contrast, Gomes writes, we in the Western Christian church give roses at baptism. Gomes continues, "We Christians, therefore, like those Greek Orthodox babies, ought to expect trouble, turmoil, and tribulation as the normal course of life. We don't, however; and we have been seduced by a false and phony version of the Christian faith which suggests that by our faith we are immune to trouble."

Draw a large cross on a piece of paper. On the vertical beam list the ways in which you are called to bear the cross. On the horizontal beam list the gifts of God given to us through faith to overcome the trials and tribulations that are a part of life.

Closing Prayer
Recite the Lord's Prayer, recalling that many—including people on the hijacked planes—found comfort and courage in this ancient prayer given to us by Jesus when the disciples asked him to teach them how to pray.